RECORD BREAKERS

at the

SUMMER OLYMPIC GAMES

**For Ma and her never-ending patience in helping
me with my English essays and vocabulary at school**

First published in Great Britain in 2024
by Welbeck Children's Books
An imprint of Hachette Children's Group
Text copyright © Rob Walker 2024
Design copyright © Hodder & Stoughton Limited

Welbeck Children's Books
An imprint of Hachette Children's Group
Part of Hodder & Stoughton Limited
Carmelite House, 50 Victoria Embankment
London EC4Y 0DZ

An Hachette UK Company
www.hachette.co.uk
www.hachettechildrens.co.uk

10 9 8 7 6 5 4 3 2 1
ISBN 978 1 8045 3564 6

Printed and bound in Guangdong, China

Writer: Rob Walker
Cowriter: Alex Rice
Senior Commissioning Editor: Suhel Ahmed
Design Manager: Matt Drew
Picture Research: Paul Langan
Production: Melanie Robertson

ROB WALKER

RECORD BREAKERS

at the

SUMMER OLYMPIC GAMES

FOREWORD BY

SANYA RICHARDS-ROSS

CONTENTS

FOREWORD

SANYA RICHARDS-ROSS

Former USA track-and-field athlete and World and 2012 Olympic champion in 400m

No matter how talented they are, every single Olympian in history will have overcome difficult times on their way to glory at the Games. I am no exception.

After making the Olympic 400m final and winning a relay gold as a teenager at Athens 2004, many people thought I would win the individual track title four years later. I won the US Trials that year and set the fastest time in the heats and the semifinals at Beijing 2008. I was undefeated all season over 400m (which is 1,312 ft.) and was favorite in the final.

The race started well and I was in front after 300 meters (984 ft.), but over the last 100 meters (328 ft.) I slipped down to third, losing to two athletes who I had beaten multiple times earlier in the year. It felt like I had been denied my destiny.

But the mark of a great champion—in life and sport—is not what you win but how you bounce back from disappointments. The following year

I became World champion and then London 2012 provided my third and perhaps last chance to win gold in the 400m. This time I ran the perfect race, beating the defending champion to finally achieve the biggest goal of my life.

No matter who you are or where you live, don't ever let anyone talk you out of a dream, whatever it may be. The journey to get there can be as satisfying as the achievement itself.

Paris 2024 will be a wonderful spectacle—I cannot wait to be there, commentating for NBC.

Use this book to learn about all the different Olympic sports and prepare to be amazed by the talent, determination, and heart of every single Olympian lucky enough to have taken part at the Games.

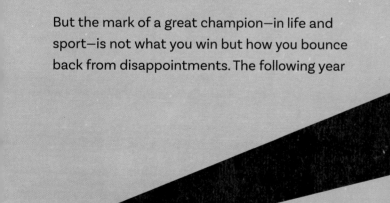

Sanya Richards was all smiles when she won the 400m finals at the US Trials to qualify for the 2008 Beijing Games.

INTRODUCTION

Whether you are watching your first, tenth, or fifteenth Olympics, the magic of the Games is sprinkled over all of us at the start of every edition as we watch the world unite for a 16-day-long celebration of the human spirit.

The fittest, strongest, and most dedicated and determined young competitors representing more than 200 countries entertain and inspire us over an amazing summer of sporting brilliance.

And if we are excited, imagine how the athletes must be feeling? Some of them may only be a few years older than you, and during the previous Olympics they, too, were watching the Games with butterflies in their stomachs, daring to dream that one day it could be them competing.

Among the many amazing things about the Olympics is that it features sports for everyone—every size and shape—and every single athlete you see competing started their sport because they enjoyed it. Some of them would have realized their natural flair as soon as they began the sport, while others would have realized their special talent only after several years.

If you love a particular Olympic sport but are not sure whether you could ever be good enough to make it onto the Olympic stage as an athlete, remember there are **HUNDREDS OF DIFFERENT JOBS IN SPORT FOR PEOPLE JUST LIKE YOU.**

As you watch Paris 2024, think not only about the athletes, but of everyone else around the Games who make this incredible event possible. Maybe you could become a coach, a masseur, a sports scientist advising the team, a camera operator, a photographer, a dietitian, or, if you love talking, maybe even a television commentator.

I fell in love with the Olympics during the Los Angeles Games of 1984. I was sitting at home watching two British athletes called Sebastian Coe and Steve Cram race to gold and silver medals in the men's 1,500m race, which is almost 1 mile, in the Athletics Stadium. To me, they looked like gods. I'd never seen anyone run so fast or with that much determination. Once I realized that I wasn't quick enough to run for Great Britain in the same race, I channeled all my energy into trying to become the person in the stadium talking about those races on television.

And with some luck and a lot of hard work, that's what I do now. And when the track and field starts, I'll be just as excited now as I was when first watching the Games 40 years ago.

It doesn't matter if you are not the smartest in your class at school. If you have a passion for a sport and are willing to work hard, who knows—maybe one day you, too, could become part of the Olympic family.

Right now, it's time to tune in and get prepared to marvel at these real-life superheroes. The greatest show on earth is about to begin!

ROB WALKER

THE GAMES BEGIN

The idea of who is the strongest, who can run the fastest, or who can jump the farthest has fascinated us humans for thousands of years. And the simplest way to find out who the champions are is by holding competitions.

This early 20th-century painting depicts a race from the ancient Olympic Games.

In 1766, archaeologists discovered an important site in Greece: ancient Olympia. It was the first known sports arena in the world, dating back some 3,000 years, where the idea of the Olympic Games as we know it today was born. At the time, it featured running races, wrestling competitions, and even chariot races.

Further research led archeologists to pinpoint 776 BCE as the year the ancient Games started. They took place every four years, lasting up to five days by the fifth century. As time went on, more and more events—including women's competitions—were added to the program. Sometimes, they attracted as many as 40,000 spectators.

Despite being such a big part of life for more than 1,000 years, the Roman emperor Theodosius banned the Games in 393 CE. He didn't like some of the traditions around them and wanted people to focus on religion and faith instead.

"Citius, Altius, Fortius"

"Swifter, Higher, Stronger," Olympic motto, written in Latin.

THE FOUNDING FATHER

As archeologists learned more about the amazing site in Greece, many people started thinking about bringing the Olympic Games back to life. And with the help of one particularly passionate Frenchman, they eventually did.

Baron Pierre de Coubertin loved education and believed sport was a great way to celebrate life and build character. In 1894, he organized a big meeting in Paris where representatives from 49 sports and 12 different countries agreed that the Olympic Games should be revived.

Hosting the first modern Games wasn't easy. The Greek organizing committee sold special stamps to help raise funds and needed a donation from a wealthy businessman, but after a determined effort, on April 1, 1896, King George I of Greece declared the first Modern Olympic Games open.

In Athens 1896, a total of 245 men from 14 countries arrived in Greece to compete, setting the benchmark for the modern Olympic Games. It's amazing to think of how many incredible athletes and moments have followed in the 128 years since the first modern Games.

In Paris 2024, we will once again see the best in the world strive for these ideals in this historic sporting arena.

QUEST FOR MEDALS

The Olympics is a gigantic stage that invites countries from around the world to showcase their athletic talents. But instead of seeking ordinary prizes, the competitors are after something extraordinary—the beautiful medals that symbolize honor and prestige.

Why do nations want these medals so much? Well, medals are a symbol of a country's athletic might. When an athlete clinches a medal, the message of the country that person represents is, "we're champions on the world's grandest sports stage." It's a moment of immense pride and elation for everyone back home. Yet, there's more to it than just national pride. Medals are like passports to international recognition. When a country wins a lot of these medals, it's telling the world that it is a powerhouse in sports and it is open to friendly interactions. This can foster international friendships, attract global investments, and even boost tourism. What's more, success at the Olympics often translates to more resources for sports development, ensuring future generations have the chance to aim for greatness.

Gymnast Simone Biles added four gold medals to USA's tally at Rio 2016.

CHARTING SUCCESS

While the Olympics promote sportsmanship and unity, winning medals is the ultimate goal for countries. It is the pursuit of excellence on a global stage, where the whole world watches in awe. Here is a list* of the top 10 all-time, medal-winning countries at the Summer Olympics, from the first Games in 1896 to Tokyo 2020.

NO.	NATION	GOLD	SILVER	BRONZE	TOTAL
1	United States (USA)	1,061	830	738	2,629
2	Russia (RUS) includes: Russian Empire (RU1), Soviet Union (URS), Unified Team (EUN), Olympics Athletes from Russia (OAR), Russian Olympic Committee (ROC)	608	515	502	1,625
3	Germany (GER) includes: United Team of Germany (EUA), West Germany (FRG), East Germany (GDR)	438	457	491	1,386
4	Great Britain (GBR)	284	318	314	916
5	China (CHN)	263	199	174	636
6	France (FRA)	223	251	277	751
7	Italy (ITA)	217	188	213	618
8	Hungary (HUN)	181	154	176	511
9	Japan (JPN)	169	150	178	497
10	Australia (AUS)	164	173	210	547

*This list was correct at the time the data was collated, but changes might have occurred as a result of athletes retrospectively having been stripped of medals due to doping violations.

GREATEST MOMENTS

The Summer Olympics have produced some of the most extraordinary moments in sporting history. A lot of these awe-inspiring episodes involve athletes defying odds, smashing records, and occasionally performing an act so remarkable that it has captured the hearts of the watching world. Here are five fascinating situations that have left an indelible mark on my imagination and become part of the enduring legacy of the Games.

1996 — KERRI'S WILL TO WIN

At just 4 feet 9½ inches (1.46m) tall and weighing only 86 pounds (39kg), 18-year-old US gymnast Kerri Strug became a gigantic star at the Atlanta Games in 1996. After snapping her left ankle on her first attempt performing the vault, she somehow fought through the pain to produce a second effort, ensuring Team USA won gold in the combinedexercise. With her ankle in a cast, she was carried to the podium by her coach. Kerri's bravery made her a household name in the USA.

2020 — CHAMPIONS TOGETHER

High jumper Gianmarco Tamberi of Italy and his great friend and rival Mutaz Essa Barshim of Qatar had both recovered from career-threatening injuries before arriving at Tokyo 2020. In the men's high jump final, they matched each other jump for jump. Both utterly exhausted, the moment they realized they could share the gold medal will go down in history. Barshim was hugging people in the crowd, while Tamberi was rolling around on the track crying with joy.

1968
MESSAGE TO THE WORLD

At the 1968 Games in Mexico City, American sprinter Tommie Smith won the Men's 200m in a new world record time while teammate John Carlos came third. During the medal ceremony, they both stood barefoot, each wearing a black glove, and raised their fists above their heads. It was a gesture to show the world that the treatment of Black Americans at home was not fair and had to change. They had made their mark on the Games forever.

1992
LEAN ON ME

After withdrawing with an injury just before his Olympic heat in 1988, British 400m runner Derek Redmond was not going to let anything stop him at the Barcelona Games in 1992. But at about 492 feet (150m) into his semifinal race, he had a hamstring tear and collapsed. Before medics could get to him, his father Jim ran onto the track, picked him up, and helped Derek finish the race to a standing ovation from the crowd. Redmond said the moment made him more famous than he would be if he had won the gold medal.

1984
TRAILBLAZER ON THE TRACK

Nawal El Moutawakel made history in 1984 when she became the first Moroccan, African, and Muslim woman to win an Olympic gold medal. Her Olympic achievement in the 400m hurdles saw locals in her hometown of Casablanca pour onto the streets to celebrate. Indeed, her breakthrough inspired Moroccan women to believe in themselves and take up sport, which had previously been regarded as the preserve of men.

At Paris 2024, more than 10,500 athletes will compete in 329 medal events in 32 different sports, which will be spread across 18 magical days of competition.

Here's a rundown of all the sports at the Paris Games. The sports are ordered according to their scheduling on the Olympic program, with those lasting the longest featured first. You will get the lowdown on each sport with the aims and rules, so that you know what to expect and what to look for. Plus, we've included fascinating historical highlights from previous Games and amazing record breakers who have left their mark, inspiring the current crop of Olympians to follow in their hallowed footsteps.

OLYMPIC SPORTS

SOCCER

DID YOU KNOW?

Center midfielders cover almost 7 miles (11km) during a 90-minute game. Over the course of an Olympic tournament, a player could run more than 40 miles (66km)—not even marathon runners can match that!

Mexico beat Brazil 2–1 in the men's Olympic soccer final in London 2012.

The world's most popular sport has been part of the Olympics since 1900. The first Olympic women's tournament took place at Atlanta 1996 and was won by the hosts, USA, in front of more than 76,000 fans.

Following the rules of "Association Football," in soccer, two teams of 11 players try to score goals against each other over 90 minutes using mainly their feet. Extra time is played if the scores are level in the knockout stages. If the teams still can't be separated, a dramatic penalty shootout takes place. There are 16 teams in the men's tournament and 12 in the women's; professional players can take part, but teams in the men's tournament can have only three players over the age of 23, so spectators get to see the stars of the future with a few big names.

2008 MAGICAL MESSI

One of soccer's greatest players, Lionel Messi is an Olympic champion. He was just 21 years old when he helped Argentina beat Nigeria in the 2008 final. In 2017, he called it the win he values the most.

RECORD BREAKER

 Formiga

Brazil's Formiga played in the first seven Women's Olympic soccer tournaments. She was 18 years old when she first appeared at Atlanta 1996 and was still going strong at Tokyo 2020. She won silver at both the 2004 and 2008 Games.

JARGON BUSTER

A **POACHER** is the name given to an attacker who frequently uses speed, skills, and guile to evade defenders around the goal area and score.

1996 TRUE TO HER WORD

Before the first women's Olympic soccer tournament in 1996, USA's Briana Scurry told a newspaper that she would run naked through the streets if her team won. So when USA beat China in the final, that is exactly what she did, wearing only her gold medal. However, she did it at 2 a.m., which helped to spare her blushes.

RUGBY

DID YOU KNOW?

Rugby sevens is a professional sport played at international level, with the most prestigious competition being the World Rugby Sevens Series. The top teams at the end of the season qualify for the Olympic Games.

Kazuhiro Goya of Japan dives to score a try during the men's bronze medal final match against South Africa at Rio 2016.

Matches are 14 minutes long, featuring two halves of 7 minutes each. With just seven players in a team, scrums and line-outs are contested by three players instead of the usual eight. However, many of the normal 15-a-side rules apply; while moving forward, the ball can be passed only backward, but kicking the ball forward is fine. There are five points for a try, three for a penalty or drop goal, and two for a conversion.

Rugby sevens is the seven-a-side form of rugby union. Played on a full-size field, it is shorter, faster, and exhilarating to watch. The sport made its Olympic debut in 2016 and drew huge interest, particularly in nations less familiar with the sport.

RECORD BREAKER

🏴󠁧󠁢󠁿 🇫🇯 **Fiji**

Before rugby sevens appeared at the Olympics, Fiji had never won an Olympic medal. So, when Fiji's men beat Great Britain 43–7 in the 2016 final it was a huge deal for the Pacific Island, which celebrated the win with a national holiday. Another gold medal followed in 2020, and Fiji's women's team also made the podium, winning bronze at the same edition.

HEROES IMMORTALIZED

2016

Following Fiji's triumph at Rio 2016, the team's sponsor released a 17-minute documentary telling the story of how the humble nation became Olympic champions with their fast and powerful brand of rugby sevens.

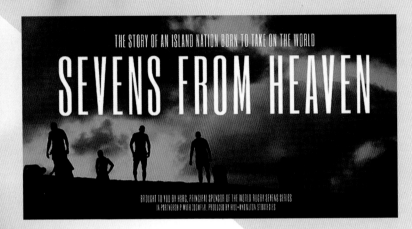

THE STORY OF AN ISLAND NATION BORN TO TAKE ON THE WORLD

SEVENS FROM HEAVEN

BROUGHT TO YOU BY HSBC, PRINCIPAL SPONSOR OF THE WORLD RUGBY SEVENS SERIES
IN PARTNERSHIP WITH 20SIXTEEN. PRODUCED BY HILL+KNOWLTON STRATEGIES

! JARGON BUSTER

A **MAUL**, or standing tackle, in rugby sevens is when one or more players from each team is bound to the ball carrier in a contest to keep or seize possession.

SIGNATURE CELEBRATION

2020

When New Zealand's women won gold at Tokyo 2020, they delighted audiences worldwide by performing a special version of their traditional dance, the *haka*. With its rhythmic movements and terrifying facial expressions, the dance is usually performed before the start of a match to intimidate the opposition—but this time it was part of a big celebration.

HANDBALL

2024 DATES
JUL 25–AUG 11

NO. OF TEAMS
24

GOLDS AVAILABLE
2

A cross between basketball and soccer, handball is a seven-a-side indoor game where the aim is to throw the ball into the other team's goal. It's much more high-scoring than soccer—the women's final at the Tokyo Olympics had 55 goals.

Handball matches are 60 minutes long and the aim is to throw the ball into a goal that is 2 meters (6½ ft.) high and 3 meters (9¾ ft.) wide (smaller than a soccer goal). Players bounce the ball like they do in basketball and can take three steps when they stop dribbling. Only the goalie is allowed in the D-shape goal area. However, players can jump into the area, which often happens when they are shooting. The results can be spectacular.

DID YOU KNOW?

Handball made its Olympic debut in 1936, but it looked very different back then. It was played outdoors and there were 11 players on each side. Germany, who invented the sport, won the sport's first gold medal.

Spain edged past Egypt 33–31 in the men's bronze medal match at the Tokyo 2020 Games.

2000 COUPLE FACE OFF

History was made at Sydney 2000 when, for the first time at the Olympics, a married couple played against each other. Norway's Mia Hundvin got the better of her partner Camilla Andersen of Denmark on the first day of competition, but it was Camilla and the Danes who came home with the gold in the final.

JARGON BUSTER

In Handball, a **DIVING SHOT** is an attempt made on goal where the attacker leaps up and hurls their body toward the goal as they shoot for maximum power.

RECORD BREAKER

Mikkel Hansen

Denmark's Mikkel Hansen is often called handball's G.O.A.T (Greatest Of All Time). With eight goals, he was the top scorer in the 2016 Olympic final, which Denmark won. Having scored 165 goals across four editions of the Games, he is the all-time leading scorer on the Olympic stage.

2008 SILVER LINING

Although Iceland lost the 2008 men's handball final to France, the team was given a heroes' welcome back home. Iceland had just become the smallest country to win an Olympic medal in a team sport and 40,000 people—12.5 percent of the country's population—lined the streets to cheer the team.

ARCHERY

The Parthenon provided a dramatic background to the archery contest at Athens 2004.

Archers aim at a target face that is divided into 10 scoring rings and five colors. They get a maximum 10 points if they hit the gold ring in the middle and just 1 point if they strike the outer white ring.

There are Individual and team events, plus a mixed team competition for men and women. All the archery events have a knockout format.

JARGON BUSTER

A **SHOOT-OFF** occurs when scores are tied at the end of the rounds. It sees each archer, or archers in the team, shoot a single arrow. The arrow closest to the center of the target wins the match.

Archery is among the oldest sports in the Olympic Games. The competition occurs outdoors with archers trying to hit a tiny target 70 meters (230 ft.) away. This sport takes incredible physical and mental strength.

RECORD BREAKER

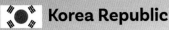 **Korea Republic**

The most successful archery nation on the Olympic stage is Korea Republic. They have finished top of the medal's table at every Olympics since 1988 and won four of the five events at Tokyo 2020. They practice hard to be the best—it's estimated that Korea Republic's Olympic archers shoot 125,000 arrows a year!

DID YOU KNOW?

The oldest female Olympic champion is American archer Eliza Pollock, who was 63 years old when she won team gold at the 1904 Games.

2020 SANSATIONAL!

Korea Republic's An San shot herself into the history books by winning her third gold medal, in the women's Individual event, at Tokyo 2020. Already a double gold medalist in the women's recurve team and mixed team competition, San became the first athlete of the Games to win three gold medals—and the first archer in the sport's modern history to crest three podiums at a single edition.

2020 VIRTUAL BEST

Turkey's Olympic champion Mete Gazoz, who won the men's Individual gold in Tokyo, is just as good in the virtual world. He won an Olympic e-sports archery competition, playing the game Tic-Tac Bow.

AQUATICS

How many Olympic sports can you think of that use water? Aquatics has five of them: swimming, diving, water polo, artistic swimming, and marathon swimming. Let's start with swimming, which is a huge part of every Olympic Games.

SWIMMING

Swimming has featured in the Olympics since the first edition in 1896. Back then, races took place in the sea, but the waves were a problem and organizers soon switched to swimming pools. An Olympic pool is 50 meters (164 ft.) long and has eight lanes.

There are four different swimming strokes: freestyle, backstroke, breaststroke, and butterfly. Freestyle, wich is usually the front crawl, is the fastest. Races range in distance from 50m to a lung-busting 1,500m—that's almost 1 mile, or 30 lengths of the pool. Swimmers often compete in several races. For example, at Tokyo 2020, Emma McKeon of Australia competed in seven different swimming events and won a medal in each one! Swimming is only second to track and field in awarding the most medals at the Olympic Games.

JARGON BUSTER

Freestyle and backstroke swimmers do underwater somersaults known as **FLIP TURNS** at the end of each length. Flip turns enable the swimmers to push off the wall with their feet, giving them maximum speed and momentum in a race.

1952 | DAD'S SPLASH

Jean Boiteux was the first French swimmer to win an Olympic gold medal, taking the Men's 400m freestyle title in Helsinki (1952). However, that famous day is remembered more for his father's wild celebrations. Boiteux senior (Gaston) had swum for France at the Paris Olympics in 1924; Gaston was so overjoyed that Jean had finally won a gold for the country that he jumped into the pool to hug his son.

2020 | FEAR CONQUERED

When Great Britain's Adam Peaty was a boy, he would scream during bath time, because he was so scared of getting wet. His mother, Caroline, took him to swimming lessons to help him overcome his fear, and a star was born. At Tokyo 2020, Peaty became the first swimmer from his country to successfully defend an Olympic title, when he won his second 100m (328 ft.) breaststroke gold. It goes to show that even Olympic champions can find their chosen sport hard to start with.

A NEW DAWN

Australia always produces amazing swimmers. One of their most important stars is Dawn Fraser (center)—who started swimming only to help her breathing problems when she was a child. Fraser was the first Olympian in history to win gold in the same race at three successive Games (100m/328 ft. freestyle in 1956, 1960, and 1964). Most incredibly, she won the third of those golds a few months after she was involved in a car accident in which she tragically lost her mother.

DIVING

This dynamic sport is all about entering the water from a platform or a springboard. Divers perform spins, twists, and rotations in the air, and then plunge into the pool with as little splash as possible. There are also synchronized events where two divers perform exactly the same dive at the same time.

DID YOU KNOW?

Divers dry off in between dives to ensure the rate at which their body spins stays correct when they dive. The spin rate will speed up if they are soaking wet, causing them to slip out of position and ruin the timing of their entry.

Diving demands great skill and courage, especially when jumping off a 10-meter (33-ft.) platform. It's the same height as two giraffes standing on top of each other. A bouncy springboard, 3 meters (98 ft.) above the water, is used for other diving events.

Men perform six different dives and women five, with each one given marks out of 10 by a group of judges. The highest overall score at the end of the competition wins, so every dive counts.

RECORD BREAKER

 Guo Jingjing

Known as the "diving queen," China's Guo Jingjing was one of the stars of the 2008 Beijing Olympics. The springboard diver won two golds, just as she did at the 2004 Olympics. It was the first time a female diver had won back-to-back individual and synchronized Olympic titles.

GREEK SURPRISE

2004

Greece won an unlikely synchronized diving gold at the 2004 Games, when springboard pair Nikolaos Siranidis (left) and Thomas Bimis came from behind. The pair were in fourth place before the final round of dives, and it seemed inevitable that China's Peng Bo and Wang Kenan—who had never lost a major international competition together—would win. But Wang lost control on his dive, scoring no points, and the two other pairs ahead of them also struggled under pressure. The Greeks meanwhile performed a spectacular final dive to give the hosts a memorable gold.

⚠ JARGON BUSTER

Divers aim to finish with a splashless **RIP** entry into the water. It is called a rip because the smoothness of the entry sounds like someone tearing a piece of paper.

FAMOUS HEADACHE

1988

At the 1988 Games, USA Diver Greg Louganis was the defending champion in both the 3m springboard and 10m platform events. In one of diving's most infamous moments, he hit his head on the board during a qualifying dive and was bleeding when he reached the water. Instead of pulling out, he got straight back on the board—and won two golds again.

MARATHON SWIMMING

The Olympics has two marathon swimming races, one each for men and women, held outdoors over a 10-kilometer (6¼-mile) course. The race takes almost 2 hours to complete and is one of the toughest tests of strength and endurance at the Olympics. In 2008, silver medalist David Davies of Great Britain was so exhausted at the end of the men's race that he had to be carried away on a stretcher.

WATER POLO

Having first appeared in 1900, water polo is the oldest team sport at the Olympics. Women's water polo was added to the Olympic program at the 2000 Sydney Games.

A match is played between two teams of seven players. The sport resembles handball in water, with players trying to throw a ball into the opponent's goal. Players cannot touch the bottom or hang on the wall. A match is 32 minutes long, divided into four quarters, and a 30-second shot clock operates after winning possession.

2020 WET WHOOP

The USA's women's water polo team thrashed European champions Spain 14–5 in the 2020 Olympic final to win a record third successive gold medal. Team USA's coaches were so delighted with the triumph that they jumped into the pool to celebrate with the players.

ARTISTIC SWIMMING

Artistic swimming, which used to be known as synchronized swimming, involves a mixture of swimming, diving, and acrobatics as teams perform stunning routines to music.

The event features teams of eight as well as a separate duets competition. The performers must be graceful, agile, and extremely fit; it's common for swimmers to hold their breath for a minute during a routine. Like diving, each performance is marked by judges.

DID YOU KNOW?

Artistic swimmers are not allowed to touch the bottom of the pool, which makes the complicated lifts they perform even more impressive!

RECORD BREAKER

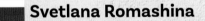

Svetlana Romashina

Russia's Svetlana Romashina is the most decorated artistic swimmer in Olympic history. Making her debut at the 2008 Games, she competed in seven Olympic artistic swimming events, which included three duet competitions, and won them all. She is the only woman to go undefeated in her Olympic career while entering seven or more events.

JARGON BUSTER

In artistic swimming, **EGGBEATER** is a term used to describe the elegant leg kicks that help swimmers tread water and keep their arms free.

VOLLEYBALL

Serbia and Korea Republic battled it out for the volleyball bronze medal at Tokyo 2020.

DID YOU KNOW?

Volleyball was invented in 1895 by an American named William Morgan, who combined elements of other sports to create his new game. He used a basketball and a tennis net and got the idea to use hands from handball.

This indoor sport is played on a court by two teams of six players, separated by a net. The aim is to hit the ball in the other half of the court without it being returned. Volleyball debuted at the 1924 Games as a demonstration sport.

Each team can touch the ball up to three times before hitting it back over the net, but the same player can't touch the ball twice in a row. Hands are normally used but any part of the body is allowed. Matches are the best of five sets, with 25 points needed to win a set, or 15 in the decider. A point is awarded to the winner of each rally, no matter who is serving. Contests that go to five sets can last more than 2 hours.

2020 GOLD AT LAST

After winning silver in both the 2008 and 2012 Games, and bronze in 2016, the USA women's team finally won their first volleyball gold medal at Tokyo 2020. "The hard work, the sweat, the tears, the blood—it's been worth it," their middle blocker Haleigh Washington said after the competition.

1964 ART IMITATING LIFE

After Japan's women won the inaugural volleyball competition in 1964, the team's success resonated across popular culture, particularly within anime (Japanese animation). The craze was capitalized on by Chikako Urano, whose manga series "Attack No. 1" followed an all-girls, high school volleyball team and became the first televised female sports anime series.

MARGARET COMICS

アタックNo.1

富士見学園の新星の巻

①

FUJIMI

浦野千賀子

JARGON BUSTER

The **SPIKE** is a powerful shot in volleyball. Hit from the net, it is a downward smash into the opponent's court. A spiked volleyball can reach up to 80 miles per hour (129km/h).

BASKETBALL

2024 DATES
JUL 27– AUG 10

NO. TEAMS
16 + 24

GOLDS AVAILABLE
4

Superstar Lebron James of the USA led the men's team to gold at the 2012 Games in London.

DID YOU KNOW?

In the 3x3 format, basketballs are one size smaller than the size 7 balls used in normal basketball to suit the faster pace of the game.

Basketball is hugely popular and some of the sport's greatest have starred at the Olympics, including Michael Jordan, Magic Johnson, and LeBron James. There's now also a three-a-side version at the Olympics—3x3 basketball.

The aim of basketball is to dribble and pass the ball downcourt and shoot it into the opponent's basket. A successful shot is worth two points, or three if it is made outside the 6.75-meter (22-ft.) line. Each team has five players and games are played in four periods of 10 minutes each. In the 3x3 version, basketball is played on a half-court with one basket. A successful shot is worth 1 or 2 points and the winner is the first to score 21 points, or whoever is ahead when the 10 minutes are up.

EVERY SECOND COUNTS

1972

The final in the 1972 Munich Games saw the USA's long unbeaten run of 62 matches ended by the Soviet Union, who scored the winning basket in the last second. It was a hugely controversial win—the USA had celebrated victory at full time before an official ordered the clock to be put back.

JARGON BUSTER

A **TIME-OUT** in Basketball is a period of 60 seconds, during which the play is stopped and teams discuss strategy while players have a moment to rest and take some fluids.

TITANIC WIN

1976

Female basketball star Uljana Semjonova dominated the 1976 Olympics. The 7-foot 1-inch (2.16m)-tall center averaged 19 points and 12 rebounds per game for the Soviet Union women's team. With Semjonova in the side, the team won gold, beating their archrival USA in the final.

RECORD BREAKER

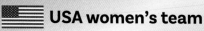 **USA women's team**

Olympic women's basketball is dominated by the USA. The team won their seventh consecutive Olympic title at Tokyo 2020 and clinched the inaugural 3x3 basketball gold, too.

BEACH VOLLEYBALL

2024 DATES
JUL 27– JUL 10

NO. TEAMS
48

GOLDS AVAILABLE
2

Unlike indoor volleyball, Beach Volleyball has just two players per team. Each side has up to three touches to get the ball back over the net into the other team's half, and the rally ends when the ball goes out or isn't returned. Matches are the best of three sets; each set is the first to 21 points apart from the deciding set (if needed) in which the first to 15 points wins the match.

Chile's Esteban Grimalt performs a diving move called a dig at the 2016 Games to keep the ball from touching the sand.

Included since 1996, beach volleyball is a big hit with the crowds. The sun, sand, and loud music give the sport a carnival atmosphere. However, it's not always played on a beach—the venue for Paris 2024 is the Eiffel Tower.

DID YOU KNOW?

The ball used in beach Volleyball is inflated to a 30 percent lower air pressure than that used in indoor volleyball. This makes it move slower through the air, making it easier for the two players covering the court.

FAMILY FORTUNE

Norway's Olympic champion Anders Mol (circled) first celebrated with his family after he and Christian Sørum (center) won gold at Tokyo 2020. Anders' father Kaare coaches the pair, while his uncle Jetmund and mother Merita, an Olympian herself, were also part of the support team.

RECORD BREAKER

Kerri Walsh Jennings

USA's Kerri Walsh Jennings won 26 consecutive Olympic beach volleyball matches across four editions of the Games, from Athens 2004 to Rio 2016—a record for an individual female. Kerri had two partners during this time: April Ross and Misty May-Treanor.

1996

DOMINANT DUO

Beach volleyball made its Olympic debut at the 1996 Atlanta Games. USA and Brazil shared all the gold medals in the subsequent four editions, except in Sydney, where the Australian women's team triumphed.

JARGON BUSTER

The term **HUSBAND-AND-WIFE** describes a momentary loss of communication between teammates that results in the ball dropping on their side of the court.

BRASIL
ANA PATRICIA

2 USA

BOXING

This combat sport has been a big part of the Olympics for more than 100 years, but women first competed only in 2012. It is one of the most popular Olympic sports—81 nations sent boxers to take part at the Tokyo 2020 Games.

Boxers compete in three-round bouts, with each round lasting 3 minutes. The bouts take place in a boxing ring which measures 6.1 meters on each side. Five judges score the bout and decide the winner, who then progresses to the next round. Eventually two boxers fight for the gold medal, and bronze medals are awarded to each losing semifinalist. There are lots of different weight divisions, from Flyweight to Super-Heavyweight.

JARGON BUSTER

Punches count only when landed cleanly to the front of a fighter's head or to their midsection. These are the official **TARGET AREAS** in Olympic boxing.

DID YOU KNOW?

At Tokyo 2020, Ireland's Aidan and Michaela Walsh became the first boxing brother and sister to compete at the Olympics. Aidan, the younger of the two, won a bronze medal in the men's welterweight division.

1996

TRUE G.O.A.T

One of the greatest-ever boxers, Muhammad Ali, is an Olympic champion. He won the light-heavyweight gold in Rome in 1960, when he was known as Cassius Clay (see page 117). In 1996, he was chosen to light the cauldron during the opening ceremony of the Atlanta Olympics.

RECORD BREAKER

Cuba

Although the USA is the most successful boxing nation, Cuba comes second, which is an incredible achievement for a country with a population of just above 11 million. At the 1992 Games, seven Cuban boxers won gold medals!

1972

TRUE PATRIOT

After Cuban boxer Teófilo Stevenson bulldozed his way to heavyweight gold in 1972, boxing promoters clamored for the Cuban to turn professional, but Stevenson believed passionately in the Cuban Revolution and preferred to fight on behalf of his country. When asked about all the money he turned down, he often replied, "What is $1 million against eight million Cubans who love me?"

TABLE TENNIS

Matches are the best of five or seven games, with 11 points needed to win a game. If the score reaches 10-10, play continues until a player or team wins by two clear points.

All competitions have a knockout format—at Tokyo 2020 the mixed doubles event appeared for the first time, joining the men's and women's singles and team competitions.

Also known as Ping-Pong, table tennis was invented in the 1880s as an indoor version of tennis. Two or three shots are hit every second with a small plastic ball traveling at speeds up to 70 miles per hour (112km/h). Table tennis made its Olympic debut in 1988.

Some players from the East hold the bat in the "penholder" grip.

DID YOU KNOW?

The 2004 table tennis competition included the athlete with the shortest name in Olympic history— People's Republic of Korea's O Il, who competed in the men's singles event.

RECORD BREAKER
Ma Long

At Tokyo 2020, China's Ma Long became the first table tennis player to win five Olympic gold medals in his career. He is widely regarded as the sport's greatest player.

JARGON BUSTER

A **CHOP** is a defensive shot used to return a ball with plenty of backspin. It is done by brushing the ball with the bottom of the paddle in a downward motion.

2020 — WINNING CLINCH

One of the most intense celebrations at Tokyo 2020 came in the mixed doubles event, when Japan's dynamic duo of Jun Mizutani and Mima Ito beat Chinese pair Xu Xin and Liu Shiwen in the final. It was the first gold for any non-Chinese players since 2004. Mizutani gave his partner such a strong hug that she had to push him away, because it was hurting.

1992 — IN THE NICK OF TIME

Doubles champions Lu Lin and Wang Tao used up more energy than usual to win their gold medal at the 1992 Games. The Chinese pair were forced to run to the venue when their shuttle bus failed to show up at the Olympic Village. They arrived just in time to play their German opponents and, somehow, found the energy to win a five-game thriller!

2024 DATES
JUL 27– AUG 10
COMPETITORS
318
GOLDS AVAILABLE
18

Artistic gymnastics challenges gymnasts to perform intricate, acrobatic moves on apparatus including the beam, vault ,and floor. Rhythmic gymnastics is a female-only event that incorporates dance and music into the sport; gymnasts perform with hoops, balls, clubs, and ribbons. Trampolining sees gymnasts propel themselves 10 meters (33 ft.) up in the air—twice the height of an adult female giraffe. All events are scored by judges.

RECORD BREAKER
 Simone Biles

Simone Biles was a teenager when she wowed viewers at Rio 2016 by winning four gold medals—the most at a single Games by a US gymnast. The 4-foot 8-inch (1.42m)-tall athlete won gold in the floor exercise, vault, all-around, and team event, living up to her billing as one of gymnastics' all-time greats.

DID YOU KNOW?

At the 1996 Games, each individual men's competition was won by a different nation, the first time that had ever happened. Athletes from China, Greece, Germany, Ukraine, Switzerland, Italy, and Russia all claimed gold.

Gymnastics has three Olympic disciplines: artistic, rhythmic, and trampolining. Artistic events is the best known and has been a major part of every Olympic Games. All three require grace, strength, balance, and incredible skill.

1976

COMANECI IN COMMAND

At the 1976 Montreal Olympic Games, Romanian gymnast Nadia Comaneci became the first gymnast in Olympic history to be awarded a perfect score of 10.0 for her performance on the uneven bars. The official Olympic scoreboard couldn't display the score, because the manufacturers didn't think such a score was possible!

2020

FOUR TOPS

Dong Dong of China became the first trampoline gymnast to win four medals in four Olympic Games when he took silver at Tokyo 2020. The London 2012 champion decided to retire after his latest success, appropriately for a trampoline gymnast, he ended on a high.

DID YOU KNOW?

Rings were a part of the gymnastics program in the first modern Olympic Games in Athens in 1896. Ioannis Mitropoulos from Greece won the first gold medal in the event.

2016 RHYTHMIC RUSSIAN

At Rio 2016, Russia's Margarita Mamun emerged as the new champion in the rhythmic gymnastics individual all-around final, after a pressure-filled duel with her friend and teammate Yana Kudryavtseva, topping a podium that her personal coach, and former Olympian, Amina Zaripova had just missed in 1996.

CRO	MOR	HUN	CAN	ROM	BUL
9.10	8.90	9.00	9.00	8.90	9.30

SCHERBO
BLR
9.

RECORD BREAKER

Vitaly Scherbo

Belarusian gymnast Vitaly Scherbo is the most successful male Olympian in gymnastics. At the 1992 Barcelona Games, he earned six gold medals, the most by any gymnast in a single Olympics. His incredible career boasts a total of 10 Olympic medals.

1972 FLIP THE SCRIPT

Three-time gold medalist at the 1972 Munich Games, 17-year-old Olga Korbut of the Soviet Union was the first Olympic gymnast to do a backward somersault on the beam and the first to perform a backflip to catch on the uneven bars. The latter move is now known as the "Korbut Flip."

JARGON BUSTER

A gymnast **STICKS A LANDING** when they manage to dismount (from an apparatus) or land perfectly after executing a move, without taking a backward step or stumbling.

45

HOCKEY

DID YOU KNOW?

Hockey is the only team sport to have had Olympic champions from every traditional continent.

Or officially field hockey, this sport made its debut at the 1908 Games. Played on an artificial grass field, two teams of 11 use hooked sticks to hit a hard ball toward the opponent's goal.

Matches last 60 minutes, played over four 15-minute periods, and players are estimated to run about 5 miles (8km) during a game. Both the men's and women's competitions start with group games, with the top four advancing to the quarterfinals. Unlike soccer, goals can only be scored from inside the shooting circle and there is no offside rule.

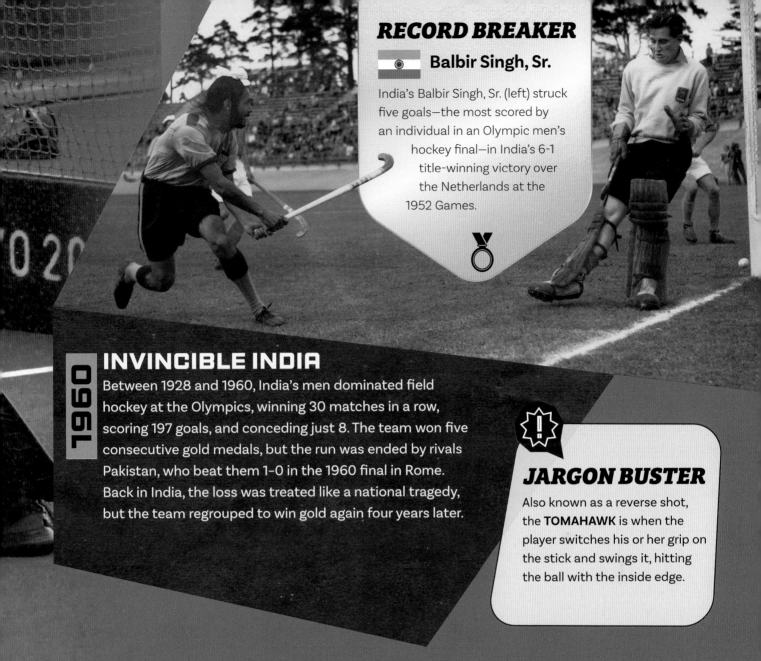

RECORD BREAKER
Balbir Singh, Sr.

India's Balbir Singh, Sr. (left) struck five goals—the most scored by an individual in an Olympic men's hockey final—in India's 6-1 title-winning victory over the Netherlands at the 1952 Games.

1960
INVINCIBLE INDIA

Between 1928 and 1960, India's men dominated field hockey at the Olympics, winning 30 matches in a row, scoring 197 goals, and conceding just 8. The team won five consecutive gold medals, but the run was ended by rivals Pakistan, who beat them 1-0 in the 1960 final in Rome. Back in India, the loss was treated like a national tragedy, but the team regrouped to win gold again four years later.

! JARGON BUSTER

Also known as a reverse shot, the **TOMAHAWK** is when the player switches his or her grip on the stick and swings it, hitting the ball with the inside edge.

2016
PERFECT PREP

At the 2016 Rio Games, Great Britain's women met tournament favorites the Netherlands, winner of the previous two titles, in the Hockey final. Despite Dutch dominance, Great Britain clung on and the match went to penalties. Step up Team GB keeper Maddie Hinch, who referred to the pre-match notes written on her water bottle to keep out every Dutch effort for a dramatic win.

EQUESTRIAN

Equestrian is an Olympic sport where women and men compete together. Dressage is a test of a rider's relationship with his or her horse, with marks awarded for routines performed in a flat, sandy area. Jumping and eventing are more action-packed; the cross-country event sees horse and rider gallop about 3¾ miles (6km) in the countryside, leaping more than 30 obstacles, including logs, water, banks, and ditches.

Equestrian events involve riding on horseback. There are three disciplines in the Olympics: dressage, eventing, and jumping (sometimes known as show jumping)—the ultimate test for an equestrian.

DID YOU KNOW?

In 2012, Canadian show jumper Ian Millar (above) became the first athlete in any sport to compete in 10 Olympic Games. Back home, he is known as "Captain Canada."

STEELY ERIC

2008

Canadian show jumper Eric Lamaze had a tough childhood, being raised in Montreal by his grandmother after his mother was jailed. At the age of 15, he dropped out of school, found a job in a stable, and worked his way up to become a rider. In 2008, he won Olympic gold on his horse, Hickstead.

JARGON BUSTER

In Dressage, a **PIROUETTE** is when a horse performs a smooth and rhythmic circle on a radius equal to its own length.

RECORD BREAKER
Isabell Werth

Isabell Werth of Germany is the most decorated Olympic rider, with 7 golds and 12 medals in total. Four of these golds came with her horse Gigolo—the pair were a dazzling dressage duo at the 1992, 1996, and 2000 Games.

STAR STALLION

1952

British horse Foxhunter became a national hero after helping Great Britain win a dramatic jumping gold by completing a clear round at the 1952 Helsinki Olympics. The horse received masses of fan mail and gifts, and there were even requests for Foxhunter's autograph after rumors spread that the horse could sign his name!

BADMINTON

2024 DATES
JUL 27– AUG 5

COMPETITORS
172

GOLDS AVAILABLE
5

RECORD BREAKER

 Lin Dan

China has won more than half the gold medals available since badminton made its Olympic debut in 1992. At London 2012, all five events were won by Chinese athletes, including Lin Dan (above), who became the first player to retain the men's singles title.

Badminton is the world's fastest racket sport, with players hitting shuttlecocks at speeds of 150 miles per hour (240km/h.) A 20-second rally can see the shuttlecock hit up to 50 times. The sport first appeared at the Olympics in 1992.

There are five badminton events: men's and women's singles, men's and women's doubles, plus mixed doubles. Matches are the best of three games—the first to 21 points wins a game—and competitions begin with group phases before progressing to knockout rounds. Unlike tennis, serves are made underarm from below the waist. Players can win a point whether or not they are serving and the player who wins the point serves next.

JARGON BUSTER

In badminton, a **NET SHOT** occurs when the shuttlecock strikes the top of the net and falls right over. Net shots are never deliberately hit, and are particularly difficult to return.

2008 FITTING WINNER

Olympic mixed doubles champion Lee Yong-dae of Korea Republic first played badminton at the age of eight, because he was told to exercise more. He soon became fit and played well. At the 2008 Olympics in Beijing, he won the mixed doubles gold as a teenager with Lee Hyo-jung and followed that up with a men's doubles medal at London 2012.

DID YOU KNOW?

The shuttlecock is made of 16 goose feathers built into a cork base. The feathers are usually taken from the goose's left wing, which is considered stronger.

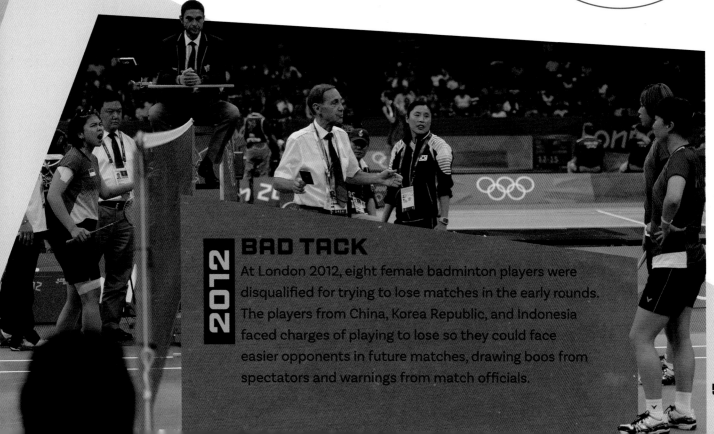

2012 BAD TACK

At London 2012, eight female badminton players were disqualified for trying to lose matches in the early rounds. The players from China, Korea Republic, and Indonesia faced charges of playing to lose so they could face easier opponents in future matches, drawing boos from spectators and warnings from match officials.

2024 DATES
JUL 27– AUG 10

COMPETITORS
199

GOLDS AVAILABLE
16

anoe sprint comprises both canoe and kayak races. In a kayak—made of a light frame with a watertight covering—the paddler is seated and uses a double-blade paddle. In a canoe—which is an open-deck craft—the paddler kneels and uses a single-blade paddle. There are singles, pairs, and fours events. Kayaks and canoes are used in canoe slalom, too, but instead of a straight sprint race, paddlers must navigate up to 25 gates on a high-octane white-water course and receive a time penalty for every gate they miss.

The canoe/kayak slalom events test a competitor's ability over a course up to 300 meters (985 feet) long.

The Games feature two types of canoe events: canoe slalom and canoe sprint. Canoe sprint sees athletes race each other on a stretch of open water, while canoe slalom is a ride against the clock on a white-water course.

JARGON BUSTER

RIDING THE WASH is when a craft gains an unfair advantage by traveling in the current, or wash, of the next boat, so that it is being "pulled along" by it.

1972
EYES ON THE PRIZE

In preparation for slalom's entry into the 1972 Olympics, hosts West Germany constructed an artificial white-water stadium costing millions. As the only facility of its kind in the world, West Germany had a real advantage in terms of training, but East Germany—determined to beat their western counterpart—sent undercover agents to map the site and secretly built a copy of the course in Zwickau. The sleuthing paid off, because East Germany destroyed all competition, taking home every single slalom gold medal.

DID YOU KNOW?

The kayak, which means "man boat" in Eskimo, originates from the icy waters off the coast of Siberia, and was primarily used as a hunting and fishing boat.

RECORD BREAKER

 Jessica Fox

Jessica Fox of Australia became the first women's canoe slalom champion when the event was introduced at Tokyo 2020. The Australian—coached by her French mother, who is also an Olympic medalist—had picked up medals at the previous two Olympics in the kayak.

FOX J.

B.BOUKPETI

2008
SNAP WIN

Benjamin Boukpeti of Togo was so excited to win a canoe slalom bronze medal at the 2008 Games that he snapped his paddle in half after his run. He had just become Togo's first Olympic medalist, so he had every reason to celebrate.

SHOOTING

Rifle and pistol shooters fire at a fixed target 10, 25, or 50 meters (33, 83, and 164 ft.) away. The target is divided into 10 scoring rings. The closer the shot is to the center of the target, the more points the shooter scores. In shotgun, competitors fire at dome-shape disks propelled through the air at speeds of 60 miles per hour(97km/h). These 4¼-inch (11cm)-diameter, pitch-and-chalk disks explode in a puff when hit.

2004
LOVE AT FIRST AIM

At the 2004 Games, USA's Matthew Emmons had a healthy lead going into the final round of his rifle final, but he accidentally fired at the wrong target. The mistake cost him a medal. There was, however, one big positive—he met his future wife, Czech shooter Katerina Kurkova, who came over to console him after the competition.

This sport is all about accuracy. Olympic shooters hit targets that are either stationary or moving, depending on the competition. There are three different disciplines: rifle, pistol, and shotgun; each feature five different events.

DID YOU KNOW?

Safety is critical in shooting. The use of safety goggles, ear protection, and proper firearm handling techniques ensure a highly secure environment.

1900

BLOODY BEGINNINGS

Can you believe pigeon shooting was an Olympic sport at the Games in Paris in 1900? The Olympian would be locked and loaded with a rifle when pigeons were released in front of him. In total, about 300 pigeons were shot dead in what must have been a bloody, feathery mess. Thankfully, pigeons were replaced by disks (clay targets) at the 1904 Games.

RECORD BREAKER

Nino Salukvadze

Nino Salukvadze of Georgia became the first woman to compete in NINE summer Olympics at Tokyo 2020. The pistol shooter, who won a gold medal at her first Olympic Games in 1988, also made history when she competed with her son Tsotne at the 2016 Games.

Shooters must have extreme hand-eye coordination and focus to succeed in the sport.

JARGON BUSTER

The **CALIBER** refers to the inner diameter of a gun barrel, which determines the size of the ammunition. The Olympics has strict rules on the caliber of firearm allowed for each event.

NOWACKA O.   KIM S.
POL   KO
384
0

FENCING

2024 DATES
JUL 27— AUG 4

COMPETITORS
212

GOLDS AVAILABLE
12

DID YOU KNOW?

The fencing suits are white because in earlier times touching was recorded with a piece of cotton, dripped in ink, placed at the tip of the weapon.

The three disciplines of modern fencing are the foil, épée, and saber. Each uses a slightly different type of blade and has its own set of rules. The sport isn't dangerous, because the tip of each weapon is covered by a metal button that triggers a light when a successful hit is made. A hit scores 1 point and the first to 15 points wins. All three disciplines take place on a rectangular area known as a *piste*, which is 14 meters (46 ft.) long and up to 2 meters (6½ ft.) wide.

Fencing is one of five sports to feature in every Olympic Games. It is a combat sport played with a special weapon, and points are scored by striking the opponent's body. Baron Pierre de Coubertin, who helped revive the Games, was a fencer.

1924 PREMIER DANE

The first female Olympic fencing champion was 33-year-old Ellen Osiier of Denmark, who won the women's individual foil at the 1924 Games in Paris. A century later, she remains Denmark's only Olympic fencing gold medalist.

RECORD BREAKER

Nedo Nadi

Nedo Nadi of Italy won five golds at the 1920 Olympics in Antwerp and his younger brother Aldo won three (all in team events with Nedo) plus one silver. The family total of nine medals in one Games is an Olympic record.

JARGON BUSTER

EN GARDE refers to the stance fencers take before combat begins. They have their rear arm curled up for balance and stand sideways, making the target area harder to hit.

BARRIER BREAKER

2016

Ibtihaj Muhammad became the first Muslim woman to represent the USA at the 2016 Games wearing a hijab. She was part of the women's saber team that won a bronze medal. That same year, *Time* magazine placed Ibtihaj on its list of "The 100 Most Influential People."

2024 DATES
JUL 27— AUG 4

COMPETITORS
250

GOLDS AVAILABLE
4

ROAD CYCLING

Road cycling is one of four cycling disciplines at the Olympics. It is a phenomenal test of stamina and team tactics, particularly the road race, which is a mass-start event raced over a long distance.

The women's road race at Tokyo 2020 saw 67 cyclists from 40 nations compete, with 48 cyclists completing the course.

Road cycling consists of two events: the time trial and road race. The time trial is a race against the clock, with cyclists setting off at 90-second intervals, while the road race is a particularly long race to the finish line. Both require immense stamina, and it's rare for a cyclist to win a medal in both. At Tokyo 2020, the road race distances were about 145 miles (234km) for men and 85 miles (137km) for women.

JARGON BUSTER

LEADOUT is a tactic in which a rider races to the front of the pack, creating a draft for the teammate following behind them, who then gains an advantage over the competition.

RECORD BREAKER

Primož Roglič

Primož Roglič claimed Slovenia's first Olympic cycling gold when he won the men's time trial at Tokyo 2020. His road to glory was an unusual one, having started out as a world-class ski jumper. He switched sports in 2012, because he felt it was time for a new challenge.

2016 KEEN CRAVEN

When race officials told Namibia's Dan Craven that he could compete in the cycling time trial event at Rio 2016 as a result of others crashing out, he said yes immediately, although he had only a road bike, not a time trial bike. Craven finished last, but he has no regrets. He later said: "I love my country ... I can say I competed in an Olympic time trial."

1984 BLADES TO SADDLE

The first women's road race champion at the Olympics, Connie Carpenter-Phinney, competed in speed skating at the 1972 Winter Games in Sapporo when she was just 14 years old. It was 12 years later when the American won Olympic gold as a cyclist at the Los Angeles Games, beating her nearest rival by less than half a wheel.

JUDO

This Japanese martial art made its Olympic debut at the 1964 Games in Tokyo. Judo translates as "gentle way," but don't be fooled—the aim is to throw the opponent to the ground with force and speed.

RECORD BREAKER

 Japan

Unsurprisingly, Japan is the most successful judo nation. The country has won more golds in Judo than any other sport and dominated at Tokyo 2020, winning 9 of the 15 events.

Men and women compete in seven weight categories. Contests are held on square mats called *tatamis* and last up to 5 minutes for men and 4 minutes for women. A bout is won instantly by *ippon*, which is scored when an opponent is thrown on his or her back or pinned to the floor for 20 seconds. Otherwise, the winner is the *judoka* with the most points at the end of the bout. In the event of a tie, a "golden score" period gets underway, where the first *judoka* to score wins the contest.

JARGON BUSTER

After *ippon*, the next highest score is **WAZA-ARI**, which is awarded for a controlled throw. Two *waza-ari*—awarded for a throw that isn't good enough for *ippon*—also ends the contest.

DUTCH DESTROYER

1964

It was a moment of national pride when Japan introduced Judo to the global arena at the 1964 Games. However, it was Dutchman Antonius Geesink who defied home expectations by winning the open event.

TERRIFIC TANI

1996

One of the smallest champions is Japan's Ryoko Tani, who won medals at all five of the Olympic Games she competed in, despite standing just 4 feet 9 inches (145cm) tall. After a surprise defeat in the 1996 Olympic final, she responded by going a whole 12 years unbeaten at international level and became an icon in her homeland.

SUPER TED

2020

Although Japan has won the most medals in judo at the Olympic Games, the most titled *judoka* in the world is Teddy Ringer—the French heavyweight *judoka*. He is a three-time Olympic champion who was undefeated in 154 bouts between 2010 and 2020. The 6 foot 8-inch (203cm)-tall heavyweight is nicknamed "Teddy Bear," but he is neither soft nor cuddly on the mat.

DID YOU KNOW?

Judo was invented in 1882 by Japanese martial artist Kanō Jigorō. He introduced Judo to Europe during a visit in 1889.

ROWING

Did you know rowing is the only race where athletes cross the finish line backward? A part of every Olympics since 1900, rowing would have featured in the first Games had it not been canceled due to bad weather.

Rowers propel boats with oars while facing in the opposite direction. They race against each other over a distance of 2,000 meters (6,560 ft.), with up to six crews in each race. There are two types of events: sculling, where competitors hold an oar in each hand, and sweep rowing, where one oar is held with both hands. The men's and women's eights are the only races to have a "cox" in the boat. The cox, who doesn't have an oar, faces forward and is responsible for race strategy. In the modern Games, there is an even split of seven men's and seven women's events.

1996
WONDROUS WIN

After winning his fourth gold medal at the 1996 Olympics, an exhausted Steve Redgrave (right) of Great Britain said, "If anyone sees me going near a boat again, they have my permission to shoot me." Four years later, he was back in a boat winning Olympic gold medal number five! His achievement is even more remarkable given that he was diagnosed with diabetes in between those Games.

2008 — TWINS STRIKE TWICE

Identical twin sisters Georgina and Caroline Evers-Swindell of New Zealand won gold in the double sculls at Athens 2004 and Beijing 2008, becoming the first duo to defend a title in the discipline. They beat Germany by just a hundredth of a second in the 2008 final, taking the lead for the first time as they crossed the line!

RECORD BREAKER

Jack Beresford

Jack Beresford of the USA won medals in five consecutive Olympic Games, including gold in the doublesculls in 1936, making him one of the most successful rowers of all time.

TENNIS

Some of tennis' biggest stars have competed at the Olympics. Among them, Roger Federer, Steffi Graf, Rafael Nadal (above), and the Williams sisters have all claimed gold since tennis returned to the Olympic program in 1988.

DID YOU KNOW?

There are eight basic tennis shots. They include the serve, forehand, backhand, volley, half volley, overhead smash, drop shot, and lob.

Tennis is a racket sport that requires power, precision, and stamina. There are different types of court surfaces, which can impact the style of play. The London 2012 tournament was played on grass at Wimbledon; hard courts were used in Rio 2016 and Tokyo 2020; Paris 2024 will use the clay courts of Stade Roland Garros, which will stage five tennis events: men's singles and doubles, women's singles and doubles, and mixed doubles.

The sport has a unique scoring system. A player scores 15 when they win a point, 30 when they win two, and 40 when they win three. A fourth point wins the game, unless the score is tied 40–40 (known as deuce), when a player must then win by two points. Matches are the best of three sets, and the first to six games wins a set.

2016
PUPPY POWER

Puerto Rico's Monica Puig caused a major upset when she won the women's singles title at Rio 2016. It was her country's first Olympic gold medal, but perhaps it was meant to be. A few months earlier, Puig had got a new puppy and named him Rio.

1920
SUPER ALL-ROUNDER

Great Britain's Max Woosnam, who won a gold and a silver medal at the 1920 Olympics, was an incredible sportsman. Not only was he an Olympic tennis champion but he also captained England and Manchester City at soccer and scored a century at Lord's Cricket Ground.

JARGON BUSTER

A **DOUBLE BAGEL** refers to a perfect 6–0 6–0 scoreline. Perfect if you are the winner, that is! Otherwise, a day you would never want to repeat in your professional career.

RECORD BREAKER
Williams sisters

The Williams sisters, Venus (left) and Serena, have both won four gold medals—three doubles titles and a singles title each. Venus has also won a silver medal in the mixed doubles, which makes her the most decorated tennis Olympian of all time.

SAILING

Each sailing event has 10 or 12 races, with points awarded for the finishing position. The lower the score the better—one point is awarded to the winner, two to the crew finishing second, and so on. The worst race score for each crew is discarded. At the end of the series, the top 10 boats go through to the medal race where points count double. The crew with the lowest overall score wins gold. The 10 events at Paris 2024 include windsurfing, kite, dinghy, and skiff for both men and women, and dinghy and multihull comprise the two mixed events.

Sailing features a series of races between boats that require one- or two-person crews. Paris 2024 will feature 10 different events, each using a specific type of sailboat, including the traditional Laser, 470, and 49er.

DID YOU KNOW?

Kiteboarding will be making its debut at Paris 2024, following a successful Olympic debut at the Youth Olympic Games in 2018.

2008 KIND RIVALS

When Denmark's Jonas Warrar and Martin Kirketerp broke their mast before the start of the 49er medal race at the 2008 Beijing Olympics, they quickly borrowed a boat from the Croatian team, who showed true Olympic spirit by helping the Danes. The Danes finished seventh in the race, which was good enough to give them the gold medal overall. "In an hour, we went from the darkest place ever to the happiest place ever," a grateful Kirketerp said.

2008 ALGAE ATTACK

On the eve of the 2008 Beijing Games, organizers had to remove more than a million ton of algae from the Olympic racecourse in Qingdao after a giant bloom left the area covered in a green film.

1960 ROYAL STAMP

After Crown Prince Constantine won gold in the dragon class event at the 1960 Games—scoring Greece's first yachting medal—the country issued a stamp to commemorate Crown Prince Constantine's victory.

RECORD BREAKER
🇬🇧 Giles Scott

The Finn dinghy made its final Olympics appearance at Tokyo 2020, which is disappointing for Great Britain, whose sailors have won every Olympic Finn event this century! Giles Scott won the final two gold medals, following on from Ben Ainslie, who won three in a row.

ΕΛΛΑΣ ΔΡ. 2.50

MOUNTAIN BIKE

Mountain biking takes place on a steep off-road course. The bikes are designed for the hilly terrain of the race, which takes about an hour-and-a-half to complete. The sport has been a big hit since it made its Olympic debut in 1996.

Great Britain's Tom Pidcock tears down a hill on the Izu Mountain Bike Course at the Tokyo Games in 2020.

Mountain bikers require great endurance, plenty of strength, and exceptional bike-handling skills. There's a men's and a women's race, each featuring 36 cyclists tackling the course at the same time. The first cyclist to pass the finish line wins. The number of laps of the course is only decided the day before the first race, determined by the weather and course conditions.

RECORD BREAKER

Julien Absalon

France is the most successful mountain biking nation at the Olympics. Julien Absalon won back-to-back titles in 2004 and 2008; in Athens he was cheered on by a group of 70 fans from his hometown and his wife, Emilie, who fainted in the intense heat just before her husband crossed the finish line.

2020

GUTSY RIDERS

Jolanda Neff of Switzerland won the women's cross-country gold at Tokyo 2020 less than two years after a horrific crash that left her with a ruptured spleen, a fractured rib, and a collapsed lung. The men's champion in Tokyo, Tom Pidcock of Great Britain, had broken his collarbone just two months earlier. His coach called his gold medal win "mission impossible."

! JARGON BUSTER

BROWN POW refers to the grippy loam and slightly damp soil that make for the optimal ground conditions for riding.

? DID YOU KNOW?

The speed record for a mountain bike is 166 miles per hour (268km/h). This was achieved by Eric Barone in the French Alps on a snowy ski slope in 2017.

2008

MENTAL LOCK

After winning a surprise Olympic medal ahead of fellow countrywoman and favorite Alison Sydor at Athens 2004, Canada's Marie-Hélène Prémont came into the 2008 Games as the favorite herself. However, in a later television interview, she admitted to being unable to sleep the night before the race, worrying about something going wrong. She ended up retiring from the race after experiencing hyperventilation.

TRIATHLON

Races begin with a mass start, with athletes diving into open water from a pontoon. The clock keeps running as athletes switch from swimming to cycling, which is why changeover speed is so crucial and sometimes called the fourth discipline. The 10km run is where stamina is tested as athletes race to cross the finish line first. The mixed-relay event features four athletes per team, with each athlete completing a 300m (985- ft.) swim, 7.4km (4½-mile) bike ride, and 2km (1¼-mile) run.

Triathlon is a multisport event that tests endurance. Athletes start with a 1.5km (4,900 ft.) swim outdoors, switch to a 40km (25-mile) bike ride, and end with a 10km (6¼-mile) run. The event requires a lot of skill when going from one event to another.

RECORD BREAKER

Flora Duffy

Bermuda became the smallest country to win gold at a Summer Games when Flora Duffy triumphed in the women's triathlon at Tokyo 2020. Did you know the distance covered in a triathlon race is longer than the length of Bermuda?!

DID YOU KNOW?

The first Olympic triathlon, held in Sydney in 2000, was watched by 500,000 spectators over the two days.

JARGON BUSTER

After completing the swim portion of a triathlon, getting onto the bike quickly is a real skill. A **FLYING SQUIRREL MOUNT** involves running with the bike while attempting to jump over the saddle and begin pedaling in a single, fluid move.

2016 PARA-TROOPER

Michellie Jones (below right) of Australia—who won a silver medal in the first women's Olympic triathlon in 2000—won a gold medal at the 2016 Paralympics as the guide for para-triathlete Katie Kelly. She described it as the best thing she had ever done.

2016 SIBLING RIVALRY

Great Britain's Brownlee brothers, Alistair and Jonathan, were on the podium together at London 2012 and Rio 2016. Alistair won gold both times, with his younger brother saying in 2016, "I'm used to getting beaten by him!"

At Tokyo 2020, Great Britain's Charlotte Worthington won the freestyle event.

CYCLING BMX

BMX cycling has two Olympic disciplines: racing and freestyle. Racing contains thrills and spills over a daunting 400m (1,312-ft.) course; freestyle is full of spectacular air, transfer ,and jump tricks. It has been described as "gymnastics on a bike."

In BMX racing, the racers launch themselves down an 8-meter (26-ft.)-high start ramp and charge around a 400m course containing jumps, tight bends, and other obstacles. The racing is fast and furious. BMX freestyle, which made its Olympic debut at Tokyo 2020, is just as thrilling to watch. Each athlete has 60 seconds to impress judges with a series of their best tricks; marks are awarded for difficulty, originality, execution, height, and creativity.

RECORD BREAKER
Niek Kimmann

The Dutch cyclist was a record breaker (and a bone breaker) at Tokyo 2020. He became the Netherlands' first BMX Olympic champion and, incredibly, he did it with a fractured knee after crashing into a steward during a training run.

2020
PRICE OF GOLD

Logan Martin became the first BMX Olympic freestyle champion when he won gold at the Tokyo 2020 Games. The Australian didn't have a training facility near his home, so he built one in his own backyard. It proved to be $70,000 (AUD) well spent!

DID YOU KNOW?

BMX stands for "bicycle moto-X" and started in the 1970s as a cycling version of a dirt bike racing sport known as motorcross.

2016
NATION'S BELOVED

Colombia's Mariana Pajón became known as the "Queen of BMX" after winning the BMX racing gold at London 2012 and Rio 2016. Colombia built a major BMX facility to honor their Olympic hero—the Mariana Pajón BMX Supercross Complex—which staged the 2016 World Championships. Unsurprisingly, Mariana won, to the delight of her home fans.

JARGON BUSTER

If you hear the terms **SPINES**, **WALLS**, and **BOX JUMPS** at the Olympics, you are at the BMX Freestyle. These are the names of some of the obstacles cyclists use to execute tricks.

2024 DATES
AUG 1— AUG 11

COMPETITORS
1,810

GOLDS AVAILABLE
48

SPRINTS, RELAYS, AND HURDLES

At every Olympics, it is the sprints, relays, and hurdles that often light up the track. These events showcase the blazing speed, teamwork, and agility of athletes, who have spent years training for their moment of glory.

Sprint events cover distances of 100m (328 ft.), 200m (656 ft.), and 400m (1,312 ft.) with dramatic relays over 100m and 400m and hurdle races over 100/110m (360 ft.) and 400m. Many sprinters say the key for running a great race is staying as relaxed as possible and focusing on your own race. But that can be hard to do. There is little time to correct mistakes in these events, and conquering nerves is as important as being fast.

Track and field is a sport that traces its roots to events featured in the ancient Greek Olympics. The modern program includes 48 track-and-field events involving running, jumping, throwing, or walking.

⚠ JARGON BUSTER

A **FALSE START** means an athlete has been judged to have begun moving before the starting gun has fired. Unfortunately, a false start almost always leads to an instant disqualification.

BOLT UNLACED

2008

Jamaica's Usain Bolt won the first of his eight Olympic sprint gold medals over 100m in Beijing 2008. Not only did he win the gold, but he also broke the world record. And it was only in the television coverage afterward that viewers realized one of his shoelaces had been undone during the race!

DID YOU KNOW?

The first Olympic race took place in Greece in 776 BCE. The track was a little more than 180 meters (590 ft.) long, compared to today's standard track of 400 meters.

LATE TO THE RACE

2020

The 110m hurdles winner at the 2020 Games, Hansle Parchment, almost never made it to the start line for his semifinal when he boarded the wrong bus to get to the Olympic Stadium. He had to beg a Games volunteer for some money to get a taxi to the venue and arrived just in time to warm up for the competition.

MIDDLE, LONG DISTANCE, AND STEEPLECHASE

The sprints may be the fastest races to watch at the Olympics, but the middle- and long-distance events have also produced some of the greatest and most dramatic stories in the history of the Games.

Middle-distance races of 800 meters (2,625 ft.) and 1,500 meters (4,920 ft.) on a track are run close to flat out and runners need to show great tactical awareness as well as speed. The long-distance events of 5,000m (3 miles) and 10,000m (6¼ miles) require stamina, as does the 3,000m (9,840 ft.) steeplechase, which also tests runners' ability to hurdle wooden barriers and a water jump on every lap.

2000 RACE TO THE LINE

One of the best distance races ever seen was the Men's 10,000m final at the Sydney Olympics in 2000. Ethiopia's Haile Gebrselassie and Kenya's Paul Tergat repeated their gold and silver from the Atlanta Games of 1996, but the race was so close there was a smaller winning margin than there had been in the men's 100m (328 ft.) final at the same Games! Just 0.09 of a second separated them after they raced for more than 6 miles!

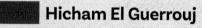

RECORD BREAKER

Hicham El Guerrouj

Morocco's Hicham El Guerrouj is considered one of the best middle-distance runners of all time. After setting the world record of 3:26:00 for the Men's 1,500m in 1998, he managed silver at the 2000 Games but made an epic return in 2004, winning gold in both the 1,500m and 5,000m races.

JARGON BUSTER

The term **BOXED IN** during a race describes a runner who is stuck in the middle of a tightly bunched group of runners and has no easy way to get out.

DID YOU KNOW?

Steeplechase runners clear 28 barriers and 7 water jumps during the race. This equates to 4 hurdles and a water jump per lap after the first lap.

1920 FLASHY JUMPER

At the 1920 Antwerp Games, Great Britain's Percy Hodge won the men's 3,000m steeplechase title by more than 20 seconds. He was such a good hurdler that he used to give exhibitions where he cleared the barriers while carrying a tray, bottle, and glass full of liquid without spilling a single drop!

JUMPS AND VAULTING

Jumping and vaulting may sound straightforward, but the high jump, long jump, triple jump, and pole vault are among the most technically challenging events on the Olympics' Athletics program.

DID YOU KNOW?

The best pole vaulters in the world can maneuver their bodies above the equivalent height of an adult giraffe!

The long jump requires explosive speed, flexibility, and power, plus the timing to hit the takeoff board perfectly. The high jump is also a test of power and flexibility—the athlete must time both correctly to clear the highest vertical height. The triple jump is a three-phase movement of a hop, a step, and a jump into the sand. The pole vault is perhaps the most technical, demanding speed on the runway, and the strength and bravery of a gymnast to catapult from a pole and clear a bar several yards above the ground.

1984 KING CARL

American Carl Lewis is a track-and-field icon, whose tally of nine Olympic gold medal includes four in the long jump. At the 1984 Games, not only did he win the gold with a leap of 8.54m (28 ft.), but all of his jumps exceeded 8.50m (27½ ft.). In fact, Lewis achieved 65 consecutive victories in the event over a span of a decade—one of the sport's longest undefeated streaks.

JARGON BUSTER

The **J APPROACH** in the high jump sees an athlete running in a straight line before curving his or her run into the jump.

RECORD BREAKER
Javier Sotomayor

Holding the world record of 2.45m (8 ft. ½ in.) since 1993, Cuba's Javier Sotomayor is considered the best high jumper of all time. He broke the first world record in 1988 when he cleared a height of 2.43m, (7 ft. 11½ in.), but a Cuban boycott meant he could not go to the Olympics. But he won gold at the 1992 Games. Sotomayor is the most prolific 2.40m (7 ft. 10½ in.) jumper in history clearing the height 17 times.

1924 ENDURING LEGACY

At the 1924 Paris Games, American student William DeHart Hubbard became the first black athlete to win gold in an individual event by leaping 7.44m (24 ft. 5 in.) in the Men's long jump. Fast-forward to 24 years later in London, USA's Alice Coachman (left) won the women's high jump to become the first black woman to secure an historic title.

THROWING

The throwing events are part of the field disciplines in track and field alongside the jumps and pole vault. The Olympics showcases the best throwers in the world in the shot put, javelin, discus, and hammer.

Throwers are among the biggest athletes at an Olympic Games, but don't be fooled. It's not just about their size and power. They also need superfast footwork and great timing to be able to launch their projectile and themselves into Olympic history. The shot put, discus, and hammer are all thrown from a small circle. In contrast, javelin throwers run up across the track to gain speed before the release.

THAT'S MY GIRL

2016

At the 2016 Games, American shot putter Michelle Carter beat reigning Olympic champion Valerie Adams of New Zealand with her sixth and final throw of the competition. It was the best single throw of her entire life, setting a national record. It also ensured she went one better than her father and coach Michael Carter, who had won silver in the men's shot put at the 1984 Olympics. What a family!

JARGON BUSTER

In discus and hammer, the **CAGE** is the protective structure surrounding the throwing area. Because athletes use turns to generate momentum before throwing, a safety cage is necessary to stop wayward efforts from flying into the crowd.

CUPID STRIKES

At the 1956 Games in Melbourne, a couple of Olympic champions from different countries met, fell in love, and needed their governments' permissions to get married. Czechoslovakia's Olga Fikotová won the women's discus, while USA's Harold Connolly took gold in the men's hammer. Despite their different views on a lot of subjects, both countries agreed the wedding should be allowed. A crowd of 40,000 people watched the ceremony in Prague.

RECORD BREAKER

 Al Oerter

 USA's Al Oerter is the most accomplished athlete in the men's discus, winning the gold medal four times in consecutive Games, securing his first at the Melbourne Games in 1956. A year later, he almost died in a car accident, which makes his achievements thereafter even more special.

JAN THE MAN

After returning from a career-threatening injury, 1992 Olympic men's javelin champion Jan Železný faced intense competition at the 1996 Games. With the odds seemingly stacked against him, Železný achieved a world record-breaking distance of 88.16m (about 289 ft.) with his first throw in the final to secure a second consecutive gold. A third gold in 2000 solidified his status as a legendary javelin thrower.

MARATHON AND WALKS

Some medals in track and field are won in seconds; others take hours. The marathon and race walks are the ultimate tests of endurance. Decathletes and heptathletes, meanwhile, contest multiple events over two grueling days.

The marathon (42.5km/almost 26½ miles) and race walks (35km/21¾ miles and 20km/almost 12½ miles) offer a lot of drama, because the lead can change many times while athletes try to apply tactics to win the race. The decathlon (men) and heptathlon (women) test athletes' all-round abilities in track and field. Men complete in 10 events, finishing with a 1,500m (4,921 ft.) run, while women compete in 7 events that end with an 800m (2,625 ft.) race. Their performances in all events over two days are marked in points, and it is the overall combined points total that determines the medal winners.

RECORD BREAKER

🇸🇪 Carolina Klüft

Athens 2004 saw Sweden's Carolina Klüft become the youngest heptathlon champion in history, with the biggest winning margin ever recorded—more than 500 points. At the age of only 21, she had completed a remarkable hat trick of global titles, after winning world junior gold in 2002 and world senior gold in 2003.

BRISK BENOIT

The first women's Olympic marathon took place at the 1984 Los Angeles Games. A lot of effort had gone into convincing organizers to allow women to compete over this iconic distance, and the race was a hugely exciting and emotional moment for distance running. USA's Joan Benoit was a worthy winner—she was greeted by an incredible reception from the home crowd, when she entered the stadium leading by 400 meters (1,312 ft.).

The decathlon and heptathlon see athletes compete in the following events over two consecutive days.

DECATHLON

DAY 1	100m sprint	Long jump	Shot put	High jump	400m sprint
DAY 2	110m hurdles	Discus throw	Pole vault	Javelin throw	1500m run

HEPTATHLON

DAY 1	100m hurdles	High jump	Shot put	200m sprint
DAY 2	Long jump	Javelin throw	800m run	

(!) JARGON BUSTER

In the marathon, the term **NEGATIVE SPLITS** means that athletes have run the second half of the race quicker than the first. This strategy helps the runners to manage their energy and pace themselves, so they can speed up and overtake others toward the end of the race.

BEATING THE HEAT

British 50km (31-mile) race walker Donald Thompson prepared for the sweltering heat of the Rome Olympics in 1960 by putting on heaters and kettles in his bathroom and training with the door sealed closed. The method worked! He won gold in a new Olympic record time of 4 hours 25 minutes, and the Italian press gave the 5-foot 5-inch (165cm)-tall math teacher the nickname "Little Mouse."

GOLF

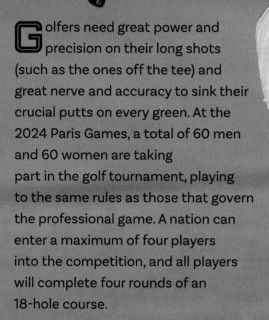

Golfers need great power and precision on their long shots (such as the ones off the tee) and great nerve and accuracy to sink their crucial putts on every green. At the 2024 Paris Games, a total of 60 men and 60 women are taking part in the golf tournament, playing to the same rules as those that govern the professional game. A nation can enter a maximum of four players into the competition, and all players will complete four rounds of an 18-hole course.

2020 BATTLE FOR BRONZE

If there is a tie for a medal-winning position, a sudden-death playoff occurs to determine the podium placings. At Toyko 2020, Pan Cheng-tsung of Chinese Taipei had to beat seven other players to secure a dramatic bronze in the men's golf, after having already played four full rounds.

Golf first appeared in the early editions of the Games but was canceled in 1908. Its return came more than a century later at the Rio Olympics in 2016. The competition inspired a carnival atmosphere around the course.

JARGON BUSTER

The term **PAR** refers to the number of shots a golfer is usually expected to take to complete each hole. That number can range between three and five.

2016
PARK CREATES HISTORY

South Korea's Inbee Park won the gold medal in the women's event at the 2016 Rio Games to become the first female Olympic champion since 1900. Following her win, Park said in an interview, "I have won many tournaments, but I have never felt this before."

DID YOU KNOW?

Terms such as "birdie," "eagle," and "albatross'"describe when a player has finished one, two, or three shots under par, respectively, on a hole.

1904
NOBLE FUNSTER

Golfers can be a lot of fun. For the St. Louis Games (1904) in the USA, 46-year-old Canadian George Lyon traveled south and told jokes, sang songs, and did handstands for the crowd on his way to becoming an Olympic champion. Four years later, he arrived at the London Games as the only entrant but turned down a guaranteed second gold on principle.

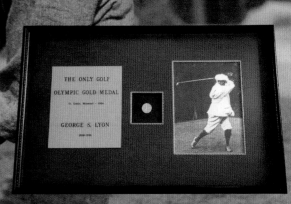

THE ONLY GOLF
OLYMPIC GOLD MEDAL
St. Louis, Missouri — 1904
GEORGE S. LYON
1858-1938

WRESTLING

The aim in wrestling is to throw an opponent to the ground, hold his or her shoulders to the ground, or outscore the other wrestler in a bout. In Greco-Roman style, wrestlers cannot target their opponents' legs or use his or her own to try to score. There are six weight divisions for men in Greco-Roman and six for both men and women in freestyle. Each bout is made up of two 3-minute periods with a 30-second break in between. The best four wrestlers in each division are seeded and the rest are drawn at random. A straight knockout system determines the medals.

JARGON BUSTER

Wrestling uses a scoring system called **THE CRITERIA** to decide the winner when scores are tied at the end of a bout. "Criteria" elements judges look at include: "technical superiority," "total points xcored," "most points in a single move," and "caution points" (penalties accrued).

Wrestling sees competitors grappling for glory. The Games feature two wrestling styles: Greco-Roman and freestyle. The former has been part of the modern Games since 1896 and is one of the oldest sports in the world.

AGAINST THE ODDS

1984

At the 1984 Games, American wrestler Jeff Blatnick produced an incredibly emotional gold medal-winning moment in the Greco-Roman superheavyweight final seven years after his brother had passed away in a motorcycleaccident and just two years after he himself had undergone extensive treatment for cancer. His uncontrollable sobbing on the mat after winning a dramatic bout drew letters of love and support from all over the world.

DID YOU KNOW?

At 412 pounds (187kg), USA's Chris Taylor (left) was the heaviest wrestler to appear at the Olympics. The superheavyweight grappler won bronze at the 1972 Games.

RECORD BREAKER

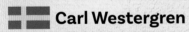 **Carl Westergren**

 Swedish wrestling sensation Carl Westergren won three golds in Greco-Roman over a glittering 12-year Olympic career from 1920 to 1932. The bus driver won titles at middleweight (1920), light-heavyweight (1924), and heavyweight (1932) and invented a move painfully known as the "lateral gut wrench." Ouch!

FAMILY FORTUNES

2020

Two Japanese sisters both tasted glory in wrestling on successive days at Tokyo 2020, when Yukako Kawai won the Women's 62kg (about 137 lb.) freestyle title on her Olympic debut and 24 hours later her sister Risako Kawai successfully defended her 57kg (about 125 lb.) crown from Rio. It's an amazing sporting double by one family.

CYCLING TRACK

The Olympic track cycling program consists of several individual and team races for both male and female cyclists. The sprint involves high-speed, head-to-head races; the keirin sees riders following a motorized pacer before sprinting to the finish. The omnium is cycling's version of the decathlon, with cyclists competing for points in four different events. Team pursuit and team sprint showcase group dynamics, and the madison is a tag-team race that is full of drama and riveting to watch.

Track cycling demands explosive power—in fact, track sprinters can reach speeds of up to 50 miles per hour (80km/h) and are well known for their strong thighs. However, good balance, technique, and tactics are also key in the pursuit of Olympic gold.

Track cycling is held indoors on a steeply banked oval track in an arena known as a velodrome. The sport featues multiple events and is a must-watch event for fans of fast-paced, high-stakes competition at the Games.

2012 ALIEN INSPIRATION

Great Britain's six-time Olympic champion Chris Hoy took up cycling as a young boy after watching the BMX chase scene in the movie *ET*. That was his "wow" moment, he says—and he himself would go on to create several wow moments by winning gold at Athens 2004, Beijing 2008, and London 2012. He is a true legend of track cycling.

DID YOU KNOW?

Track bikes don't have brakes. To stop, cyclists have to slow down the forward momentum of their legs until they can push back against the pedals.

RECORD BREAKERS

Laura and Jason Kenny

Great Britain is the most successful nation in track cycling, and in recent years husband and wife Laura and Jason Kenny have led the way. The pair have won 12 Olympic gold medals between them.

1992

FLYING THE FLAG

When Estonia's Erika Salumäe won the women's sprint at the 1992 Games in Barcelona, it was a special moment for her country, which had recently regained independence. Unfortunately, the Estonian flag was mistakenly raised upside down during the medal ceremony, but Salumäe just smiled and said they would get it right the next time. Sure enough, several Estonian athletes have followed in Salumäe's footsteps and won gold.

2020

VALUABLE LESSON

Sprint cyclist Sarah Lee Wai-sze (right) is the only Hong Kong athlete to have won medals at two Olympic Games, standing on the podium at London 2012 and then at Tokyo 2020 after crashing out in the keirin at Rio 2016. The secret of her success? Getting beaten! "I actually think losing is better than winning, because you can identify what to improve on," she says. This is great advice for all budding athletes.

JARGON BUSTER

KEIRIN is Japanese for "racing cycle." The event, which was developed in Japan, sees riders follow a "moped" called *derny,* which gradually increases in speed from 30km/h to 50km/h (about 18½ to 31 miles per hour) before exiting the track, leaving the cyclists to sprint for victory.

FINDING A WAY

There are no velodromes on the Pacific island of Guam, but that didn't stop the nation from entering a track cycling team in the 1992 Games. The Guamanian cyclists trained in a parking lot instead, and although they came last, they achieved their dream of competing at a Summer Olympic Games in 1992, when they raced in the stunning *Velodrom d'Horta* (below) in Barcelona.

RECORD BREAKER

 Anna Meares

 As well as winning six Olympic medals across four different Games from 2004 to 2016, Anna Meares of Australia won 11 world titles—making her the most decorated female track cyclist of all time. In 2021, she was inducted into Sport Australia's Hall of Fame

WEIGHT LIFTING

RECORD BREAKER

Prapawadee Jaroenrattanatarakoon

At the 2008 Games in Beijing, Thailand's Prapawadee Jaroenrattanatarakoon set two records in winning gold. Her 120kg (about 265-lb.) lift was the heaviest clean and jerk lift ever witnessed in the featherweight division, and with 31 letters, her name—which means "Good Girl, Prosperous"—was the longest ever for an Olympic champion.

Competitors have three attempts to lift as much weight as they can in two different types of lifts, and the sum weight from both determines who wins. In the "snatch," the competitors must lift the bar above their head in a single movement. In "clean and jerk," the athletes lift the bar in two movements—up to the chest in the first phase and then above the head for the second phase. There are five weight classes for both men and women at Paris 2024. Watch out for the amazing facial expressions on athletes as they strain every muscle in their bid for gold!

With its origins dating back thousands of years, weight lifting is among the purest tests of strength of all Olympic sports. Men's events have been contested since 1896, while women began competing at the Sydney Games of 2000.

DID YOU KNOW?

Tokyo 2020 superheavyweight champion Lasha Talakhadze (above) of Georgia lifted 265kg (about 584 lb.) in the clean and jerk—equivalent to a baby grand piano, motorcycle, or an adult lion.

A HERO'S WELCOME

After winning silver at Rio 2016, Hidilyn Diaz captured gold in the women's 55kg (121¼-lb.) category at Tokyo 2020, becoming the first Olympic champion from the Philippines. She was congratulated by the country's president and legendary boxer Manny Pacquiao, received a government reward of $200,000, and a heroic reception on her return home.

JARGON BUSTER

Lifters are put into **WEIGHT CLASSES** according to their body weight. This ensures fairness, because athletes compete with those of similar size. Men's Olympic weight classes range from 61kg to 109kg+ (134½ lb. to 240 lb.+), while women's are from 49kg to 87kg+ (108 lb. to about 192 lb.+).

GOOD JOB, HARRY

When USA's Harold Sakata won silver in the light-heavyweight category at the London Games of 1948, few could have predicted what would happen next. He went on to become a successful professional wrestler known as "Tosh Togo," and even greater fame followed when he starred opposite Hollywood actor Sean Connery playing famous villain Oddjob in the iconic 1964 James Bond movie, *Goldfinger*.

The combatants, known as *taekwondoins*, face off in an octagonal area measuring 8 meters (26¼ ft.) in diameter. The aim is to outscore the opponent by landing blows on the opponent's head and torso using both hands and feet. Points are earned for punches using the knuckle, and kicks using the foot or ankle. Taekwondo is fast paced and famous for its amazing-looking kicking combinations. At Paris 2024, men and women will contest in eight weight divisions, with each bout made up of three 2-minute rounds.

JARGON BUSTER

The **PROTECTIVE SCORING SYSTEM (PSS)** registers points for kicks when magnets in competitors' socks connect with sensors in their opponents' head guards or torso protectors.

Taekwondo is a great Korean martial art that has been practiced for thousands of years. The first World Championship was held in 1973 and the sport's first full medal appearance in the Olympic Games came at Sydney 2000.

DID YOU KNOW?

Taekwondo is a three-part Korean word. *Tae* means "to step on," *kwon* to fist or fight," and *do* translates as "the way or art of." As well as kicks and punches, the martial art features jabs, chops, and choking moves.

CRUCIAL KICK

Rio 2016 saw one of the most dramatic finishes to any final when Cheick Sallah Cissé won Côte d'Ivoire's (Ivory Coast's) first gold in Olympic history with a spectacular reverse turning kick in the last second of the Men's 80kg (176 lb.) showdown against Great Britain's Lutalo Muhammad. The impact back home was instant. He later reflected: "Young Ivorians recognized themselves in me. I went from being an ordinary athlete to becoming an icon and a role model."

Combatants wear protective gear during a taekwondo bout.

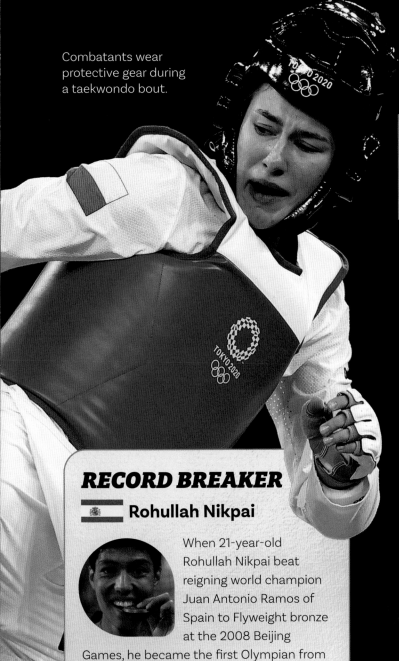

KICK-ASS CLAN

In Beijing 2008, a US. family made history by becoming the first and only trio of siblings to win individual Olympic medals at the same Games. On August 21, brother and sister Mark and Diana Lopez took silver and bronze respectively in the men's and women's featherweight divisions, and the next day their older brother Steven followed up the golds he won at Sydney 2000 and Athens 2004 with bronze in the men's welterweight division. They were all coached by their oldest brother Jean Lopez—a remarkable family effort.

RECORD BREAKER

Rohullah Nikpai

When 21-year-old Rohullah Nikpai beat reigning world champion Juan Antonio Ramos of Spain to Flyweight bronze at the 2008 Beijing Games, he became the first Olympian from Afghanistan to win a medal at any Games. He said his achievement was a message of peace to his country.

MODERN PENTATHLON

Modern Pentathlon is the true test of an athlete's abilities, involving fencing, swimming, horse riding, shooting, and running. It is held over four days, with the shooting and running events combined into a "laser run."

odern pentathlon first took place at the Stockholm Games in 1912, with women joining the program at Sydney 2000. Recent rule changes for Paris will make it exciting. After an opening fencing ranking round, days two to four will see semifinals and finals unfolding in just 90 minutes of action, with points awarded for show jumping, a bonus fencing round, 200m (655-ft.) swim, and finally a laser run, in which athletes stop to shoot five targets en route. The overall leader has a head start on the run based on the points they've accumulated from the previous events. The first to cross the finish line is the champion.

DAY 1	Ranking round	**DAY 1 EVENT** Fencing ranking and elimination round with electric épées
DAY 2	Men's semifinals	**DAY 2-4 EVENTS** • Equestrian • Fencing bonus round • Swimming 200m • Laser run
DAY 3	Women's semifinals	Men's final
DAY 4	Women's final	

LUCKY LARS

At the Helsinki Games of 1952, Sweden's Lars Hall benefited from two lucky moments en route to gold. First, the horse he was given for the horse-riding event was lame, but the replacement turned out to be the best horse in the country. Second, he arrived late for the shooting event, but because the start had been delayed, he was allowed to continue. Four years later he won again, becoming the first man in history to successfully defend the title.

Athletes shoot targets 10 meters (33 ft.) away. They try to score five hits within 50 seconds.

DID YOU KNOW?

Legend has it the events in the modern pentathlon are based on a journey made by a nineteenth-century French emissary. En route, he had to ride a horse, fight with a sword, swim, shoot, and run.

RECORD BREAKER

 Sheila Taormina

Sheila Taormina's 19th place finish in the 2008 Games saw her become the first American woman to compete in three different Olympic sports. After swimming to gold in the 4x200m (656-ft.) relay in Atlanta 1996, she switched to triathlon for Sydney 2000 and Athens 2004, before competing in the modern pentathlon at Beijing 2008.

BEST OF BRITISH

At Toyko 2020, Great Britain produced an amazing golden double, taking both men's and women's Olympic titles. Joe Choong only started the sport after watching his brother Henry take part, and he became the first British man to win gold. Kate French finished fifth at Rio 2016, but she was in sparkling form four years later, winning with a big enough lead to savor the moment in Tokyo.

NEW SPORTS

SKATEBOARDING

Skateboarding was invented in the 1950s as a way of keeping surfers entertained when the waves were flat. The sport made a spectacular entry into the Olympic Games at Tokyo 2020. Viewers were treated to street and park competitions as young stars seized their chance to shine.

Athletes in both the park and street competitions are judged on their most impressive tricks, with speed, difficulty, execution, and style all scoring points. Park events are staged on a large, bowl-shape concrete course with steep curves, enabling skaters to soar up to 3 meters (100 ft.) in the air. Street courses can be just as spectacular, with skaters using obstacles, such as rails, stairs, curbs, and benches, to perform five tricks in 45 seconds.

Hosts Japan won three of the four skateboarding gold medals at Tokyo 2020.

Innovation lies at the heart of the Olympic Games. While skateboarding, sports climbing, and surfing made their official appearance at Tokyo 2020, breaking (break dance) is the newest and coolest addition to the 2024 Olympic program.

? DID YOU KNOW?

Great Britain's Sky Brown, who won an Olympic bronze medal at the age of just 13 in Tokyo, learns most of her tricks from YouTube. She has never had a skateboarding coach.

! JARGON BUSTER

The **OLLIE** is a key skateboarding trick where the skateboarder uses his or her feet to lift the board in the air. It was invented in 1978 by Alan "Ollie" Gelfand.

SPORT CLIMBING

The famous Olympic motto "Faster, Higher, Stronger" could have been written for sport climbing. Athletes scale artificial walls using fixed hand and foot holds in three disciplines: speed, lead, and boulder. It's a huge mental and physical challenge—and in the case of the speed race, it is also spectacular!

The speed race is a battle against the clock and favors athletes with explosive power. At Paris 2024, it will be a stand-alone event with one-on-one elimination rounds. The other two disciplines, boulder and lead, are combined. Boulder requires strength, flexibility, and technique as athletes attempt to climb a 4.5-meter (14¾-ft.) wall without ropes. Lead is the endurance event—athletes have 6 minutes to scale a 15-meter (50-ft.) wall. The height the climber reaches at the 6-minute mark, or the height at which he or she falls, determines the number of points collected.

Mickaël Mawem of France excelled in bouldering at Tokyo 2020.

JARGON BUSTER

The walls have routes known as **PROBLEMS**, because it takes some time working them out. Not all climbers use the same moves. The problems are different for men and women and are reset between qualification and the final.

2020

LIVE, LOVE, AND CLIMB

World champion Janja Garnbret of Slovenia scaled to Olympic gold in the women's event at Tokyo 2020 and afterward expressed her passion for the sport, "I climb because climbing is a moment where I fall in love with life," the 22-year-old explained. "When I am on the wall, nothing else matters."

SURFING

This dynamic water sport relies on big waves, which help athletes generate speed and power to pull off some impressive moves on their surfboard. The sport itself dates back hundreds of years, but professional surfing started in the 1970s and it made its Olympic debut at Tokyo 2020.

Surfers have about 30 minutes to catch the best waves possible, with each ride marked by a panel of judges. Competitiors are marked out of 10 for each wave they ride and their two best rides are counted, producing a final mark out of 20. The judges look at the degree of difficulty, innovation, and variety in the maneuvers, plus the surfer's speed, power, and flow. The opening rounds feature four surfers against each other in heats, with the top two advancing to the knockout stage. The knockout rounds are head-to-head battles between two surfers, with the loser eliminated.

DID YOU KNOW?

Surfing at Paris 2024 is being held on the French Polynesian island of Tahiti in the South Pacific, about 9,950 mils (16,000km) from Parisl. The island is renowned for its big waves.

1912 DUKE OF HAWAII

One of surfing's earliest influencers was Duke Kahanamoku, a three-time Olympic swimming champion. The native Hawaiian competed in the pool at the 1912, 1920, and 1924 Games, winning five medals in total. He was also an avid surfer, and when he was invited by the USA and Australia governments to demonstrate the sport, it became a big hit. Almost a century later, another native Hawaiian, Carissa Moore, became the first female Olympic surfing champion when she won gold at Tokyo 2020.

BREAKING (DANCE)

Breaking was a huge success at the Youth Olympic Games in Buenos Aires in 2018 and its full Olympic debut at the Paris 2024 Games is sure to be a highlight. Breaking—a competitive form of breakdancing—is a mix of urban dance and spectacular athletic moves.

Competitors (known as B-boys and B-girls) go face-to-face in solo dance battles, adapting their moves to the beat of the DJ's music. One breaker performs and then his or her opponent responds, hoping to impress the judges who award marks for creativity, personality, technique, variety, performativity, and musicality. Power moves–including windmills, the six-step, and freezes—could make all the difference in this cool sport.

DID YOU KNOW?

Breakdancing can be traced back to the 1970s, when it emerged with hip-hop music on the streets of New York. By the 1980s, the world was gripped.

JARGON BUSTER

TOP ROCK AND GO DOWN is a key part of any breaking battle. Top rock is when the athlete dances standing upright, preparing to go down to a position on the floor. It's only top rock if the athlete goes down to the floor afterward.

NAME GAME

2024

All athletes have breaking names. For example, one of the favorites in the men's competition is Shigeyuki Nakarai of Japan, aka B-boy Shigekix (above). His breaking name, Shigekix, is a type of Japanese sour candy. What would your breaking name be?

The Paralympic Games are closely linked with the Olympic Games but are a huge event in its own right. Created for athletes with a disability, they are staged every four years shortly after the Olympics and are held in the same host city. The popularity of the Paralympics is increasingly growing. More than four billion people watched the Tokyo 2020 Paralympics on television.

Some Paralympic sports, such as track and field and swimming, are well known. Other sports, such as goalball, wheelchair rugby, and boccia, are designed specifically for para-athletes. Over the next few pages, we'll take a closer look at some of the sports and sporting heroes associated with these Games.

South Africa's Ntando Mahlangu set a world record in the men's long Jump at the 2020 Paralympics.

PARAL

YMPICS

IN THE BEGINNING

The origins of the Paralympic Games can be traced back to July 1948, three years after the end of World War II, when Dr. Ludwig Guttman decided to help injured soldiers by organizing an archery competition for wheelchair athletes at Stoke Mandeville Hospital in England. He felt sports could play a part in healing their bodies and spirits. A total of 16 injured servicemen and women took part in the competition.

Over time, athletes from other countries joined in and the Stoke Mandeville Games later became the Paralympic Games, with Rome hosting the first Paralympics in 1960. A total of 375 athletes from 21 countries competed in those Games in sports, such as wheelchair racing and swimming. These games showed that everyone, no matter their impairment or disability, could be a champion.

DID YOU KNOW?

The word "Paralympic" was created using the Greek preposition "para" (meaning beside) and "Olympic." It conveys how the two Games are run side by side.

Dr. Ludwig Guttmann is greeted at Haneda Airport ahead of the Tokyo Paralympic Games in 1964.

British athlete Margaret Webb competes in the Javelin event at the second International Stoke Mandeville Games in 1953.

As the years passed, the Paralympic Games grew bigger and better. New sports were added, including cycling, powerlifting, shooting, and wheelchair tennis. The Games have become a global celebration of incredible athletes from all walks of life. Athletes, such as Tatyana McFadden, a wheelchair racer, and Jonas Jacobsson, a sport shooter, have shown the world that disabilities are no barriers to striving for excellence. More than 75 years on, the movement has grown greatly, and 4,400 athletes from 180 nations are expected to compete at Paris 2024.

Sweden's Jonas Jacobsson triumphs in shooting at the 2008 Paralympic Games.

DID YOU KNOW?

Among the eight sports in the inaugural 1960 Paralympic Games was snooker. The cue sport was a part of the Games until 1988, but it hasn't appeared since.

PARALYMPIC SPORTS

The 2024 Paralympic Games will take place from August 28 to September 8 and will feature 22 different sports.

ARCHERY

DEBUT: 1960 GAMES

Athletes shoot arrows at a target 70 meters (330 ft.) away in both standing and wheelchair competitions.

TRACK AND FIELD

DEBUT: 1960 GAMES

Track races feature across a range of distances, plus field events that involve throwing and jumping.

BOCCIA

DEBUT: 1984 GAMES

Game in which athletes throw, kick, or use a ramp to propel a ball onto the court with the aim of getting closest to a "jack" ball.

CYCLING: TRACK/ ROAD CYCLING

DEBUT: 1984 GAMES

Races and time trials featuring bicycles, handcycles, tricycles, and tandem bikes, too.

EQUESTRIAN

DEBUT: 1996 GAMES

Paralympics features dressage-only horse-riding events, which see the ultimate test of a rider's relationship with the horse.

SOCCER 5-A-SIDE

DEBUT: 2004 GAMES

Created for soccer players with visual impairments who use a ball with a bell inside.

GOALBALL

DEBUT: 1980 GAMES

Three-a-side game for visually impaired athletes who try to throw the ball into their opponent's goal.

JUDO

DEBUT: 1988 GAMES

Tactical martial art that rewards fighters for throws and holds.

PARA-BADMINTON

DEBUT: 2020 GAMES

Indoor racket sport played by wheelchair and standing athletes, with a half court used for some matches.

PARACANOE

DEBUT: 2016 GAMES

Athletes race against each other for 200 meters (656 ft.) in a kayak or *va'a* (type of canoe) on a flatwater course.

PARATRIATHLON

DEBUT: 2016 GAMES

For the all-rounder; athletes swim 750m (246 ft.) swim, cycle 20km (12½ miles), and finish with a 5km (3-mile) run.

PARA-TAEKWONDO

DEBUT: 2020 GAMES

Martial art that awards points for kicks to the body but not the head in this version.

POWERLIFTING

DEBUT: 1984 GAMES

Athletes lift weights while lying flat on their back on a specially designed bench.

ROWING

DEBUT: 2008 GAMES

Multiple races for boats of different lengths and crew sizes on a 2,000m (6,560-ft.) flat-water course.

SHOOTING

DEBUT: 1976 GAMES

Athletes shoot at targets in rifle and pistol events from distances of 10m, 25m, and 50m (330 ft., 820 ft., and 164 ft.).

SITTING VOLLEYBALL

DEBUT: 1980 GAMES

Played on small courts with low nets, this team sport is just as intense as the standing version.

SWIMMING

DEBUT: 1960 GAMES

Pool races over various distances in breaststroke, backstroke, butterfly, freestyle and medley.

TABLE TENNIS

DEBUT: 1960 GAMES

Popular indoor racket sport played on a stationary table with events for standing and sitting athletes.

WHEELCHAIR BASKETBALL

DEBUT: 1960 GAMES

Teams of five in sports wheelchairs aim to shoot a basketball into their opponent's net.

WHEELCHAIR FENCING

DEBUT: 1960 GAMES

Fencers attempt to strike their opponent with a sword while sitting in wheelchairs that are fastened to the floor.

WHEELCHAIR RUGBY

DEBUT: 2000 GAMES

A hard-hitting mixed-team sport that combines rugby, basketball, and handball.

WHEELCHAIR TENNIS

DEBUT: 1992 GAMES

Played on Olympic tennis courts, the ball can bounce twice in this version of the racket sport.

PARALYMPIC ATHLETICS

Para track and field is the largest sport at the Paralympic Games. Inside the stadium, you'll see runners with prosthetic legs, discus throwers in wheelchairs, and visually impaired long jumpers taking part with the support of sighted guides.

USA's David Brown and his guide Jerome Avery sprint to gold in the Men's 100m T11 final at the 2016 Paralympic Games.

Paralympic athletes compete against others with a similar disability (see Paralympic Classification on page 109). Track races are held over the same distances as Olympic track races, from the 100m (328-ft.) sprint to the marathon. There are six field events: high jump, long jump, discus, shot put, javelin, and club throw.

DID YOU KNOW?

Some of the most spectacular races involve "blade runners"—amputee athletes using carbon-fiber blades as prosthetic lower limbs. The 100m is one of the Games' showpiece events. Germany's Felix Streng (left) won the Men's T64 100m in a blistering time of 10.76 seconds at Tokyo 2020!

GAME CHANGER

Women's T54 wheelchair racer Chantal Petitclerc of Canada won an incredible 14 Paralympic gold medals, including five at the 2008 Games. She is now in high office as a Canadian senator. She believes the biggest barrier to people with disabilities is attitudes in society. "We need to make sure we look at individuals with no barrier, no preconceptions, no prejudice," she told the International Paralympic Committee. "It will change everything."

WHAT IS PARALYMPIC CLASSIFICATION?

To ensure fair competition so that competitors with similar levels of ability compete against each other, they are grouped into classes based on their abilities. It is like putting athletes with wheelchairs against other wheelchair athletes or swimmers with similar abilities against each other. This system is called "classification."

Special classifiers are expert judges that evaluate each athlete's disability and how it affects his or her sport. They look at aspects, such as strength, balance, and coordination. Then, competitors are assigned a class, often labeled with a letter and a number. In track and field, the letter F is used for field athletes and T used for those competing on the track. The numbers refer to the impairment. The lower the number, the greater the impairment.

For example, numbers 11 to 13 are used for track and field athletes who are visually impaired. So, a female class 11 sprinter would compete in the Women's T11 100m; blind athletes competing in class 11 wear compulsory blindfolds and run with a guide runner. In class 12, running with a guide is optional.

When you watch the Paralympics, remember that the classification system is there to make sure every athlete has a fair chance to be a true champion.

BOCCIA

Boccia (pronounced "bot-cha") is a bowling game that has been described as the world's most inclusive sport. It is played by athletes with severe physical disabilities, who compete from a wheelchair. It is one of the few Paralympic sports where men and women face each other in the same competition.

The sport is played indoors on a flat, smooth surface about the same size as a badminton court. Athletes throw or roll six colored balls as close as possible to a white target ball, known as the "jack." Points are awarded to the player with the ball nearest the jack. When four ends have been played (or six in the team event), the points are added up and the highest score wins. It's highly tactical and skillful, testing both accuracy and mental strength.

As with other Paralympic sports, there are different classifications. In Boccia, it is split into four classes, ranging from BC1 to BC4.

2020 A SPORT TO DYE FOR

David Smith (below) is the most decorated British boccia player in history and one of the most colorful! At London 2012, the BC1 athlete sported a memorable red mohawk hairstyle, at Rio 2016 he changed it to blue, and at Tokyo 2020 he retained his Paralympic title with a red-and-blue mohawk. He is a player who dazzles in more ways than one!

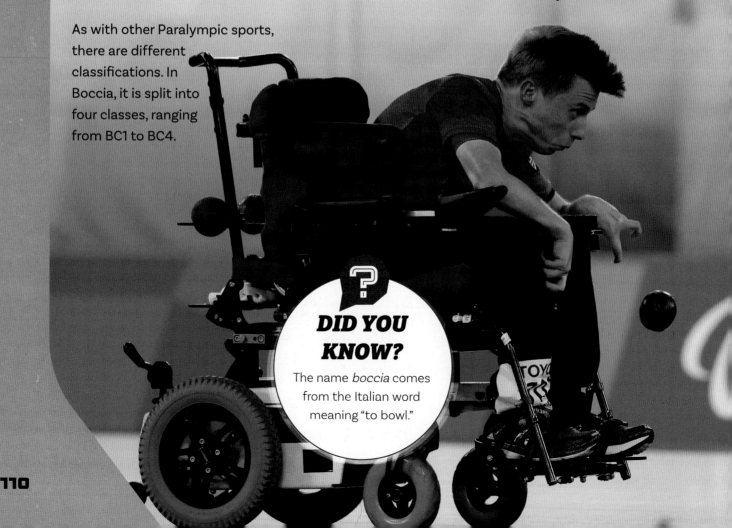

DID YOU KNOW?

The name *boccia* comes from the Italian word meaning "to bowl."

GOALBALL

Goalball is a team sport for athletes who have a visual impairment. It is played in complete silence to enable players to hear the bells in the ball, which makes it a truly different experience for spectators. However, they are allowed to cheer when a goal is scored.

? DID YOU KNOW?

During a match, the ball can reach speeds of 37 miles per hour (60km/h). Players literally throw their bodies down to stop the ball from crossing the goal line.

Goalball was invented after World War II to rehabilitate blind war veterans. It features two teams of three players, who try to bowl a hard rubber ball into their opponent's goal, which is 9 meters (29½ ft.) wide. A game consists of two 12-minute halves and to avoid time wasting, a team has 10 seconds from the time they retrieve the ball to take their shot. They can move anywhere within their team zone to throw the ball.

Throwing technique is key in this sport. Most teams release the ball near the floor so that the ball rolls silently, which makes it harder for the opposing team to hear and track it. To ensure all players are equal, blackout masks must be worn.

2020 GOALBALL G.O.A.T

Turkey's Sevda Altunoluk produced a remarkable performance in the women's final at Tokyo 2020, scoring all nine goals as her side beat USA 9-2. Sevda scored a staggering 46 goals in the competition, and she was also top scorer when Turkey won gold in 2016. No wonder she is known as the world's best player.

PARA SWIMMING

Swimming is one of the biggest sports at the Paralympic Games. It has featured in every edition of the Paralympics, with 146 medal events at Tokyo 2020. The events range from 50m (164-ft.) sprints up to 400m (13,12-ft.) endurance races across freestyle, backstroke, breaststroke, butterfly, and individual medley, plus relays.

Swimming is the only sport in which athletes with different impairments compete against each other. This is because classifications are based on the impact the impairment has on swimming instead of the impairment itself.

2020 A LONG JOURNEY

Jessica Long of the USA was adopted from Russia as a baby and had both legs amputated below the knee, having been born with a rare condition. In total she needed 25 surgeries but has overcome great odds to become a 16-time Paralympic champion! At Tokyo 2020, she won three golds, two silvers, and a bronze medal.

RECORD BREAKER

 Trischa Zorn

The most successful athlete in the history of the Paralympic Games is a visually impaired swimmer. Trischa Zorn of the USA, who was born with complete blindness, won an amazing 55 medals, including 41 golds. She competed in seven editions of the Paralympics from 1980 to 2004.

DIVINE DIAS

One of the greatest swimmers in recent years is Daniel Dias of Brazil. He retired after Tokyo 2020 with 27 Paralympic medals, including 14 golds, and was a star at his home Games in Rio. Throughout his career he was determined to improve. "I believe there is a better version of ourselves that we can search for every day and this is what continues to motivate me," he told the International Paralympic Committee. These are inspirational words for all of us.

DID YOU KNOW?

Visually impaired swimmers (classes 11–13) rely on "tappers," who use a tapping device to let them know when to turn or when they are about to approach the wall. The device is usually a pole with a soft end that is used to tap the swimmer on the head, shoulder, or back.

BLIND SOCCER

Blind soccer is played by male athletes who have a visual impairment. The five-a-side game, with two 15-minute halves, uses a special ball with a bell inside, and each team has a guide behind the opponent's goal to direct the players when they shoot.

The goalkeeper is the only member of the team who doesn't wear an eye mask. He must be sighted or partly sighted so that he can give instructions to his defenders. The field has a rebound wall running down both sides, which makes the sport fast paced. There are no throw-ins and no offside rule either, and before attempting a tackle, players must shout the word "voy" so that their opponent knows a tackle is about to be made.

DID YOU KNOW?

Brazil have won every Paralympic tournament since the sport made its debut at Athens 2004. They beat rivals Argentina 1–0 in the 2020 final to claim their fifth successive gold medal.

THE HAUL FOR BRONZE

2016

At the 2016 Games, Morocco finished last on their Paralympic debut. However, at the next Games in Tokyo, they made the podium. Zouhair Snisla (above) was Morocco's hero, scoring all four goals in their bronze medal match against China. He also finished as the tournament's top scorer.

WHEELCHAIR RUGBY

Combining elements of rugby, basketball, and handball, this is a sport so rough it was originally known as "murderball."

Wheelchair rugby is a mixed team sport for male and female athletes. It is played indoors between two teams of four in purpose-built wheelchairs, with players passing the ball to each other in a bid to cross the opponent's goal line. Big collisions between wheelchairs are a common part of the game.

Matches consist of four 8-minute quarters, and the team that scores the most goals wins. As you may have noticed, it is different from the rugby we see at the Olympics. And they don't use a rugby ball—they use a volleyball.

FROM CLUB TO COUNTRY

2020

Great Britain's Kylie Grimes won wheelchair rugby gold with Great Britain at the 2020 Games in Tokyo, the only female player in the squad. Four years earlier she had competed in track and field at the Rio Paralympics, finishing fourth in the women's F51 club throw.

CLEVER CLASSIFICATION

Players are given an official points value depending on the level of their impairment. For example, the most severely impaired athletes are graded at 0.5 point, while the most able are 3.5 points. The team points total on court at any time cannot exceed 8.0, so a team can't have its most functional athletes playing together at the same time. Wheelchair basketball has a similar classification system, which means the coaches need to be extremely tactical.

115

OLYMPIC LEGENDS

Every single Olympian is a special person with amazing determination and talent. They all deserve to be remembered, and there are some whose achievements mean even more than the medals they win or records they set. They are the legends of the Games.

1936 🇺🇸 JESSE OWENS

One of the most famous Olympians in history is American athlete Jesse Owens. At the 1936 Berlin Games, he won an incredible four gold medals over 100m (328 ft.), 200m (656 ft.), 4x100m relay, and long jump. The German leader Adolf Hitler did not like the idea of black athletes dominating sport, because he wrongly believed all humans are not born equal. But Owens' victories made a mockery of Hitler's idea of the white race being superior. In the long jump, Owens and fellow athlete Carl Ludwig "Luz" Long also showed friendship has no barriers, when the German helped his rival solve a run-up problem, although he knew it would mean silver for him behind Owens' gold. The two men stayed in touch for the rest of their lives.

OLYMPIC MEDALS
4 | 0 | 0

1960

🇺🇸 CASSIUS CLAY

At the 1960 Games in Rome, 18-year-old American Cassius Clay won light-heavyweight boxing gold with a personality and sense of humor as fast as his feet and hands. He was known for speaking up if he felt something was unfair or wrong, and after being refused service at a restaurant at home, because of his skin color, he famously threw his medal into the Ohio River. Shortly afterward, he became a Muslim and changed his name to Muhammad Ali. As a professional, he won the heavyweight world title three times and became the most famous sporting icon of all time. At the 1996 Atlanta Games, the world saw him light the Olympic flame at the opening ceremony, and at the men's basketball final he was presented with a replacement medal. The champion was rightfully reunited with his medal after 36 years.

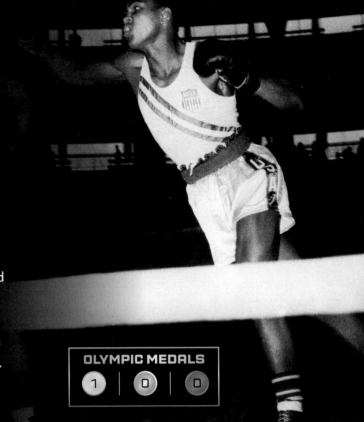

OLYMPIC MEDALS

| 1 | 0 | 0 |

2000

🇦🇺 CATHY FREEMAN

Every country hosting an Olympic Games hopes one of their athletes will deliver glory, even under the huge pressure of the home fans and televsion audiences. That was certainly the case for Australian 400m (1,312-ft.) runner Cathy Freeman at the great Sydney Olympics of 2000. A silver medalist in Atlanta in 1996, she was a two-time world champion by the time her home games arrived, and as most of her ancestors were Aborigines (the native people of Australia), she felt as if she represented all elements of her culture and country. After lighting the flame, she lit up the track, storming to gold in front of a crowd of 112,000. The noise was incredible—as was the reaction around the world.

OLYMPIC MEDALS

0
1
1

Olympic legends come from all over the world, in all shapes and sizes and in all kinds of sports. One particular quality that unites them all is determination. It is without doubt the fuel of champions.

1948 KÁROLY TAKÁCS

In 1938, right-handed Hungarian world champion pistol shooter Károly Takács had his shooting hand blown off by a grenade while serving in the army. Over the following 10 years, he taught himself to shoot with his left hand and then broke the world record and beat the favorite to win gold at the London Games of 1948. He even successfully defended his title four years later in 1952. Willpower is an incredible strength.

OLYMPIC MEDALS
| 2 | 0 | 0 |

1948  FRANCINA BLANKERS-KOEN

On the track at the London Games of 1948, experts said 30-year-old mother of two Francina "Fanny" Blankers-Koen was too old to be a contender. But the Dutch runner proved everyone wrong in spectacular style, winning the 100m (328 ft.), 200m (365 ft.), 80m (262-ft.) hurdles, and the relay. She returned home to a huge horse-drawn parade in Amsterdam. She will always be regarded as a true pioneer of women's sport.

OLYMPIC MEDALS
| 4 | 0 | 0 |

1952

 LIS HARTEL

In 1944, Danish equestrian rider Lis Hartel contracted polio while pregnant at the age of 23 and was paralyzed from the knees down. After her daughter was born, she learned to ride her horse using other leg muscles and went on to win a silver medal in Individual dressage in Helsinki 1952. The sight of her being helped onto the podium to receive her medal is regarded as one of the most emotional moments in Olympic sport, and four years later she won silver again.

OLYMPIC MEDALS
0 | 2 | 0

1996

 **GAIL DEVERS**

After reaching the 100m (328-ft.) hurdles semifinals at Seoul 1988, Gail Devers overcame two years of serious illness to make it back onto the US. Olympics team for Barcelona 1992. Despite the heartache of falling over the line in fifth after leading the final, she was destined for greatness—in her second-best event. She won the 100m sprint titles at Barcelona 1992 and Atlanta 1996, becoming only the second woman in history to successfully defend the marquee sprint title.

OLYMPIC MEDALS
3 | 0 | 0

2012

 **BEN AINSLIE**

Great Britain's Ben Ainslie enjoyed an incredible career on water, winning a silver and then four successive gold medals in two different types of boats at five editions of the Games, from Atlanta 1996 to London 2012. In winning his last title, he became the most decorated Olympic sailor in history. One of his motivations at school was to overcome bullying and prove to himself he could be good at something. And what a way to do it!

OLYMPIC MEDALS
4 | 1 | 0

PARALYMPIC LEGENDS

Above all, the Paralympics showcases the indomitable human spirit. These athletes have inspired the world not only with their talent, but also their sheer will to win, proving that physical challenges are no barriers to greatness.

2016

🇺🇸 TATYANA MCFADDEN

Tatyana McFadden was born with spina bifida (a deformity of the spine) and spent the first few years of her life in a Russian orphanage before being adopted at the age of six. Making her Paralympic debut in 2004, McFadden became one of the USA's most successful athletes, winning eight gold medals as a phenomenal T54 wheelchair racer—four of them at Rio 2016. She also won four major marathons in the same year, something no athlete had ever achieved before.

PARALYMPIC MEDALS

8	8*	4

*One of her medals came at the 2014 Winter Paralympics.

2012

🇧🇷 TEREZINHA GUILHERMINA

Visually impaired sprinter Terezinha Guilhermina of Brazil was the world number one in the Women's 100m T11 for more than a decade. She won gold in both the 100m (328 ft.) and 200m (656 ft.) at the 2012 Games and three gold medals at the following year's World Championships in Lyon, wearing her trademark colorful blindfolds. Coming from humble beginnings, she had to borrow her sister's running shoes for her first race. She finished on the podium and spent her prize money on her favorite yogurt from the local market.

PARALYMPIC MEDALS

3
2
3

2008

🇿🇦 NATALIE DU TOIT

Swimmer Natalie du Toit is one of the few athletes to have competed at the Olympics and Paralympics. The South African won 13 gold medals across three Paralympic Games and raced in the 2008 Olympic Games against able-bodied swimmers in the 10km (6¼-mile) open water marathon. Du Toit was 17 when she was hit by a car while riding a scooter to school after swimming practice. Her left leg had to be amputated, but she was determined not to give up on her dream.

PARALYMPIC MEDALS
13
2
0

2020

🇬🇧 SARAH STOREY

Sarah Storey became Great Britain's most successful Paralympian of all time when she won her seventeenth gold medal at Tokyo 2020. Five of those golds came as a swimmer at the start of her career, and 12 have come as a cyclist. On a bike, Sarah Storey is untouchable, whether on the track or road. She won four gold medals at her home Games in London in 2012 and a hat trick of golds at Rio and Tokyo. Now in her forties, she shows no sign of slowing down!

PARALYMPIC MEDALS
17 | 8 | 3

2016

🇦🇺 RYLEY BATT

Australia's Ryley Batt was born without legs, but he refused to use a wheelchair as a child, preferring to get around on a skateboard. That all changed when he saw wheelchair rugby for the first time. Batt was hooked and, as it turned out, exceptionally good. He made his Paralympic debut at the age of 15 in Athens, and he went on to inspire the Australian team to win gold in 2012 and 2016.

PARALYMPIC MEDALS
2 | 1 | 0

OLYMPIC ODDITIES

The modern Olympic movement began in 1896. That's more than a century and quarter of sporting history. In that time all kinds of strange, quirky, and wonderful things have happened. There's nothing like the Olympics!

1900

OLYMPIAN IN THE DARK

In early editions of the Games, some competitors did not understand the significance of an Olympics. For example, Luxembourg's Michel Théato won the men's marathon at Paris 1900, but he didn't realize he was an actual Olympic champion until 12 years later, when a list of records was published.

1908

ONE-MAN SHOW

At the London Games of 1908, British sprinter Wyndham Halswelle won a rerun of the Men's 400m (1,312 ft.) final on his own for a guaranteed gold. One American had been disqualified when the race was first contested and, in protest, his two teammates refused to take part second time round.

1924

SURVIVOR TAKES GOLD

Titanic survivor Dick Williams won the gold medal in mixed doubles tennis for the USA, exactly 12 years after he had leaped into freezing water, swum 100 feet (30m) to a lifeboat, and hung on all night before being rescued. He nearly had both his legs amputated, but he convinced surgeons he would recover their use.

1920

ALL-SEASON WINNER

Imagine being an Olympic champion in both Summer and Winter sports. It has happened once, when American Edward Eagan won light-heavyweight boxing gold at the Summer Games of Antwerp in 1920 and then secured winter glory at Lake Placid in 1932 in the four-man bobsled. The incredible achievement has never been repeated.

1964

FLAG LIFTER

Legendary Australian swimmer Dawn Frazer was temporarily arrested after securing her historic third successive 100m (328-ft.) freestyle gold at the 1964 Tokyo Games. She tried to steal a souvenir flag from the entrance to the Japanese Emperor's palace. All charges were eventually dropped and she was given the flag as a gift.

1952

SHOT TO GOLD

When Hungarian policeman Miklós Szilvási was accidentally shot in the left leg with a machine gun in 1946, he thought his career as a Greco-Roman wrestler was over. But he recovered to take welterweight silver in the 1948 London Games and then amazingly upgraded to gold four years later at Helsinki 1952.

2020

SPORT OR NOT?

There have been some peculiar Olympic sports, including the long jump for horses in 1900 (won by Extra Dry). More recently, hide-and-seek was put forward as an exhibition sport for Tokyo 2020. Yasuo Hazaki, head of the Japan Hide-and-Seek Promotion Committee, led the campaign but, unfortunately, it was unsuccessful.

1924

CALAMITOUS RACE

Few events have gone as badly as the 1924 cross-country race in Paris. Only 15 of the 38 runners finished the treacherous course, with record temperatures and poisonous fumes from a nearby energy plant making conditions almost unbearable. The Red Cross spent hours searching for missing athletes. Needless to say, cross-country racng never appeared in the Olympics again.

2008

NUGGET OF TRUTH

Ever wondered what the fastest Olympian eats? In his autobiography, Usain Bolt revealed that the only thing he ate during the 2008 Beijing Games was McDonald's Chicken McNuggets. His diet worked—the Jamaican sprinter won 100m (328 ft.) and 200m (656 ft.) gold in world-record times at those Games.

2012

HARTING THE HULK

Germany's Robert Harting was a discus thrower with a huge personality. After winning gold at the London Games (2012), he produced his trademark gesture of shredding his shirt for the cameras and then spent the night sleeping at a train station, because he had lost his Olympic accreditation at a party.

HOW TO BE AN OLYMPIAN

USA's Dan O'Brien was a three-time world decathlon champion and won Olympic gold at the 1996 Games. He was adopted as a baby and overcame attention deficit hyperactivity disorder (ADHD) on his way to sporting glory.

Dan O'Brien was fiercely determined to succeed after his setback at the US Olympic Trials in 1992

Mobil 1 M

Q Can you remember the first Olympics you ever watched and what inspired you about it?

A I was 13 when it happened. "The Miracle on Ice." The 1980 US hockey team beating the Russians and going on to win the Olympic gold. After the game I told my mother, "I'm going to the Olympics!" "In which sport?" she asked, and I said "I don't know." That's when the dream started.

Q Many children have ADHD and that can make school life difficult. How did you manage to overcome that?

A As a kid my ADHD went undiagnosed, because they weren't sure what it was. Classes were always hard for me, whereas sports just seem to make sense. The key to ADHD is to find the things that interest you.

Q In 1992, you failed to make the US team for the Barcelona Olympics, but a month later you broke the world record. How did you bounce back from disappointment so quickly?

A Not making the Olympic team when I was the favorite to win gold really hurt. But I had coaches, good friends, and a very supportive community. Everyone encouraged me to stay with

it, so while it hurt, I was able to get back on track and continue pursuing the goals that I set for myself.

Q What did it feel like when you crossed the finish line in Atlanta 1996 knowing you were Olympic Champion?

A It felt like the weight of the world had been lifted off my shoulders. I cried right there on the track in front of the world. It was a cry of relief. I had dreamed of winning the gold medal for years, and to experience it was truly a dream come true.

Q Life can be tough growing up as a dual-heritage American. What advice would you have for any young Americans trying to work out who they are and what they want to do?

A I was adopted at the age of two. I never met my biological parents. I had trouble fitting in at school. Sport was the key to me finding friends and figuring out who I really was. I always believed in my abilities as an athlete, and I think that helped me so much in other parts of my life that were initially a struggle for me.

INDEX

ACKNOWLEDGMENTS

To my fantastic wife Becky & my son and heir Arthur for all their patience & love and for putting up with me finishing this on our Summer Holidays in 2023!

Dad. For everything.

Sanya Richards-Ross
Becky Adlington
Sally Pearson
Dan O'Brien
Keeley Hodgkinson

Tamsin Manou
Jenny Meadows
Martin "Webby" Webster
Ernest Obeng

Mr Baker - Master of Cross Country Running at Abingdon School

Mr Trotman, Mr Mearns and Ms Soper - my English teachers at Abingdon School

Al Rice and Suhel Ahmed - without whom we wouldn't have made it to print!

PICTURE CREDITS

The publishers would like to thank the following sources for their kind permission to reproduce the pictures in this book.

Getty Images: 123T; AFP 61TR; Luis Acosta / AFP 46-47; Allsport 118TL; Odd Andersen / AFP 89TR; The Asahi Shimbun 20-21T, 45B, 72T, 87BR, 104BL; Greg Baker / AFP 20-21B; Naomi Baker 86, 115R; Scott Barbour / Allsport 112BR; Lars Baron 51TR, 54TR; Bettmann 57TR, 63B, 85BC, 87TL, 97TR, 116, 117TR, 118BR; Lutz Bongarts / Bongarts 49C; Shaun Botterill 24; Frederic J. Brown / AFP 114BL; Clive Brunskill 55R, 65BR; Ron Burton / Keystone 119TR; Central Press 83BR; Central Press / Hulton Archive 122TR; K. Y. Cheng / South China Morning Post 97R; Yasuyoshi Chiba / AFP 71BL, 113BR; China Photos 105TR; Rich Clarkson / NCAA Photos 29L, 35T; Tim Clayton / Corbis 18, 75TL; Fabrice Coffrini / AFP 78; Chris Cole / Allsport 41BL; Michael Cooper 39TR; Jim Davis / The Boston Globe 45TR; Tim de Waele 59TR, 59BR, 68T, 69TL; Adrian Dennis / AFP 80; Kristian Dowling 95BR; James Drake / Sports Illustrated 87TR; Tony Duffy 79TL; Don Emmert / AFP 67L; Express Newspapers 93BR; Jonathan Ferrey 38; David Finch 61L; Julian Finney 91B; Focus on Sport 83TL; Francolon / Simon / Gamma-Rapho 43TR; Stuart Franklin / FIFA 19R; Gamma-Rapho 76BL, 76BR; Paul Gilham 76-77; Chris Graythen 93TR; Laurence Griffiths 73TR; Jack Guez / AFP 60; Sean M. Haffey 37TL; Toru Hanai 32-33; Matthias Hangst 16-17, 82-83, 92-93; Alexander Hassenstein 123BR; Scott Heavey 121L; Julian Herbert 49TL; Tommy Hindley / Professional Sport / Popperfoto 117BL; Maja Hitij 94-95, 99T; Walter Iooss Jr. / Sports Illustrated 35BL; Yuki Iwamura / AFP 43BR; Jed Jacobsohn 27TR; Jung Yeon-je / AFP 92T; Tasos Katopodis 115B, 121BR; David E. Klutho / Sports Illustrated 19BL; Mark Kolbe 44BL; Marco Kost 99BR; Patrick Kovarik / AFP 68BR; Kyodo News 31L, 33TR, 58-59, 75BR, 101; Ed Lacey / Popperfoto 53TR; Streeter Lecka 40-41; Dickson Lee / South China Morning Post 90-91; Fred Lee 41TL; Bryn Lennon 73B; Alex Livesey 12, 48, 71BR; Andy Lyons 81BR, 82BR; Ian MacNicol 27R, 88-89; David Madison 91T, 119L; Carmen Mandato 114TR; Pierre Philippe Marcou / AFP 28BL; Maxim Marmur / AFP 62T; Bob Martin / AFP 108-109; Ronald Martinez 44-45; Clive Mason 66, 67TR, 67BR, 119BR; Leo Mason / Popperfoto 39B; Stephen McCarthy / Sportsfile 96-97; Colin McConnell / Toronto Star 85BR; Jamie McDonald 121TR; Joe McNally / Sports Illustrated 74-75C; Behrouz Mehri / AFP 95BL; Buda Mendes 112BL, 113TR; Maddie Meyer 31R; Manny Milan / Sports Illustrated 14L;

Brendan Moran / Sportsfile 26, 39TL, 52; Gray Mortimore / Allsport 15L; Dean Mouhtaropoulos 22-23, 23C, 65TL, 95TR, 102-103, 106; Dan Mullan 97BR; Koki Nagahama 107BR, 111T, 111BR; Leon Neal / AFP 36; Francois Nel 72BR; Kazuhiro Nogi / AFP 108BL; NurPhoto 42-43; Kiyoshi Ota 110; Ulrik Pedersen / NurPhoto 112-113; Tom Pennington 30BR, 57BR; Christian Petersen 34, 56-57T; Ryan Pierse 100TR; Paul Popper / Popperfoto 27B, 104-105; Popperfoto 47T, 49BR, 56BR, 62R, 65TR, 77BL, 79BL; Mike Powell 79R; Adam Pretty 29BR, 53R, 53BL; Mark Ralston / AFP 109TR; David Ramos 14BR; Peter Read Miller / Sports Illustrated 59BL; Michael Regan 50, 51B; Joe Rimkus Jr. / Miami Herald / Tribune News Service 69BR; Rolls Press / Popperfoto 15TR; Thomas Samson / AFP 64; Oli Scarff / AFP 28R; Justin Setterfield 25L, 25B; Ezra Shaw 41R, 54-55B, 61BR, 98; Diego Souto / Quality Sport Images 70B; Jamie Squire 29TR, 75TR; Michael Steele 120BR; Henri Szwarc / Icon Sport 23BR; Patrick Tehan / MediaNews Group / Bay Area News Group 37R; Marcel ter Bals / BSR Agency 30T; Bob Thomas / Popperfoto 11; Bob Thomas Sports Photography 15BR, 89BR; Topical Press Agency 122BL; Chris Trotman 84; Lucas Uebel 120L; Mauro Ujetto / NurPhoto 107TR; ullstein bild 81TR; Universal History Archive 10; Manan Vatsyayana / AFP 47B; Loic Venance / AFP 37B; Nico Vereecken / Photonews 70-71T; Phil Walter 63TR; Koji Watanabe 19TL; Jim Watson / AFP 85TL; John G. Zimmerman / Sports Illustrated 81L
HSBC Sport: 21T
Jodi Hanagan: 9
Shutterstock: More Images: (Gold texture) used throughout
Wikimedia Commons: 87BL; Chicago Historical Society 25TR; Malama Pono Ltd. 100BL; Shueisha 33BR; Stewart & Co., Melbourne 55TL

Every effort has been made to acknowledge correctly and contact the source and/or copyright holder of each picture any unintentional errors or omissions will be corrected in future editions of this book.